The American Adventure

Expansion, Conflict and Reconstruction

1825 — 1880

CONCEPTS AND INQUIRY:
The Educational Research Council
Social Science Program

ALLYN AND BACON, INC.
Boston   Rockleigh, N.J.   Atlanta   Dallas   Belmont, Calif.

The American Adventure

Expansion, Conflict and Reconstruction

1825 — 1880

Prepared by the Social Science Staff
of the Educational Research Council of America

THIS BOOK WAS PREPARED BY THE FOLLOWING MEMBERS OF THE SOCIAL SCIENCE STAFF OF THE EDUCATIONAL RESEARCH COUNCIL OF AMERICA:

THOMAS G. BERNAS, BARBARA M. BROWN, CHARLES C. BROWN, CONSTANCE BURTON, JOHN J. DWYER, JR., AUDREY B. EAGLEN, MERLE GOLNICK, MICHAEL JOYCE, JOSEPH RIBAR, RONALD M. SOBEL, ROBERT H. STEINBACH, SHERWOOD J.B. SUGDEN, JUANITA C. STOREY, MICHAEL R. SWANSON, MARLENE D. ZWEIG

AGNES M. MICHNAY, MANAGING EDITOR
MARY CATHERINE McCARTHY, EDITOR IN CHIEF
RAYMOND ENGLISH, DIRECTOR

UNIT PAGE PHOTOS
Unit V, page C-2 and C-3, *A View of San Francisco from Telegraph Hill*
Unit VI, Page C-98 and C-99, *The Battle of Mobile Bay, August 5, 1864*

The Educational Research Council of America acknowledges the contributions of the Kettering Family Fund, the Lilly Endowment, Inc., the Martha Holden Jennings Foundation, and the Scaife Family Charitable Trusts, which have made possible the Social Science Program of the Educational Research Council of America.

Cover by OMNIGRAPHICS, INC.

Printed in the United States of America

Library of Congress Catalog Card Number 74-27552

1 2 3 4 5 6 7 8 9   78 77 76 75

CONTENTS

MAPS

A NOTE TO STUDENTS

History is full of problems and controversies, and you should be prepared to argue, comment, and look up further information as you proceed. To encourage you in making original contributions, the text is interrupted by frequent questions, each identified by a symbol. The meaning of the symbols is as follows:

▶ Straightforward, often factual questions, to which there are simple correct answers.

● More complicated questions, calling for explanation and discussion. Often you will discuss these in class. You should be able to deal with these questions without doing research. Use your common sense, your logical faculty, and your broad knowledge of principles and concepts in geography, economics, political science, sociology, anthropology, psychology, philosophy, and religion, as well as history. Use your knowledge of other subjects, too, such as language, literature, art, science, and mathematics.

★ Questions requiring more information than is available in the text. You may need to do some research on these.

Enjoy the book. Use it to develop your skills in analyzing and judging human affairs.

ACKNOWLEDGMENTS

Introduction – p. C-4, (top) U.S. Department of Transportation/Federal Highway Administration, (center) U.S. Department of Transportation, (bottom) Bettman Archive; p. C-8, Library of Congress; p. C-9, (top left) Library of Congress, (bottom left) Library of Congress, (right) Historical Society of Pennsylvania; p. C-11, Boston Athenaeum, (right) H. Armstrong Roberts; p. C-12, Library of Congress; p. C-13, Library of Congress; **Chapter 1** – p. C-17, Kansas State Historical Society, Topeka; p. C-24, New York Historical Society; p. C-31, Library of Congress; p. C-35, Brown Brothers; **Chapter 2** – p. C-44, Merrimack Valley Textile Museum; p. C-46, (left top) Bettman Archive, (bottom) U.S. Department of Agriculture; p. C-50, (left) U.S. Department of Transportation/Federal Highway Administration, (right) Philadelphia Museum of Fine Arts; p. C-51, U.S. Department of Transportation; p. C-53, (left) Library of Congress, (right) Santa Fe Railway; **Chapter 3** – p. C-56, Standard Oil Company; p. C-58, (top) Library of Congress, (bottom) Smithsonian Institute; p. C-59, Granger Collection; p. C-62, Brown Brothers; p. C-63, U.S. War Department; General Staff in the National Archives; p. C-67, Library of Congress; **Chapter 4** – p. C-74, Library of Congress; p. C-80, (top) Library of Congress, (bottom) Dictionary of American Portraits; p. C-82, Library of Congress; p. C-84, Library of Congress; p. C-85, Library of Congress; p. C-96, Bettman Archive; **Unit VI**, U.S. Navy Photo; p. C-100, Library of Congress, p. C-107, Library of Congress; **Chapter 1** – p. C-108, (top left) Philadelphia Museum of Art, (top right) Metropolitan Museum, (bottom) Library of Congress; p. C-112, Library of Congress; p. C-113, Library of Congress; p. C-115, Library of Congress; p. C-117, National Portrait Gallery; p. C-118, National Portrait Gallery; p. C-120, Library of Congress; p. C-121, Library of Congress; **Chapter 2** – p. C-122, Library of Congress; p. C-125, Bettman Archive; p. C-127, Library of Congress; p. C-129, Dictionary of American Portraits; p. C-133, U.S. Signal Corps National Archives (Brady Collection); p. C-137, Library of Congress; p. C-139, H. Armstrong Roberts; **Chapter 3** – p. C-140, Library of Congress; p. C-142, Library of Congress; p. C-143, Boston Athenaeum; p. C-144, U.S. Signal Corps National Archives (Brady Collection); p. C-145, Chicago Historical Society; p. C-146, National Portrait Gallery; p. C-152, U.S. War Department General Staff/National Archives; p. C-154, H. Armstrong Roberts; p. C-155, Boston Athenaeum; **Chapter 4** – p. C-156, Library of Congress; p. C-158, American Antiquarian Society; p. C-159, (left) Dictionary of American Portraits, (right) Bettman Archive; p. C-162, Library of Congress; p. C-163, Library of Congress; p. C-164, Schomburg Collection N.Y. Public Library; p. C-165, Library of Congress; p. C-166, Bettman Archive; p. C-167, Culver Pictures; **Chapter 5** – p. C-168, Library of Congress; p. C-170, (left) Central Union Pacific R.R.; p. C-172, H. Armstrong Roberts; p. C-179, (right) Library of Congress; p. C-180, (left) Library of Congress; p. C-181, U.S. Department of Transportation/Federal Highway Administration; p. C-186, (top) Library of Congress; p. C-191, Library of Congress; p. C-192, Library of Congress.

All photographs not otherwise credited are the work of the Allyn and Bacon staff photographers.

Charts: Contis Studios
Maps: I² Geographics

Part Three

Expansion, Conflict and Reconstruction

(1825 – 1880)

Moody del. from a sketch by Swan

Unit Five

Manifest Destiny (1825–1850)

Lith. of Pewce & Pollard, San Francisco

The Iron Horse Wins in 1830

Along the Oregon Trail in 1843

A victorious Andrew Jackson on his way to Washington in 1828

Introduction
Decisions and Indecision

Accelerating Change

With the onset of the Modern Age (c. 1500), the rate of change in Western civilization speeded up. In the second quarter of the nineteenth century the process of change was still accelerating. This was evident in Western Europe. Industry was spreading. Population was increasing faster than ever before. Scientific knowledge, including the practical science of medicine, was growing. Inventions were changing technology. Democratic ideas were becoming more popular.

These accelerating changes were likewise evident in the United States. Indeed, by the end of the nineteenth century, the United States became the leading maker of changes in the world. In the 1830's, thoughtful Europeans watched the United States to see what the world of the future might be like. They did not always approve of what they saw.

The United States was a scene of turbulence and conflicting trends. It made the first experiment in modern times with representative democracy. It was aggressive and imperialistic, though Americans called their imperialism "manifest destiny." It was, more and more, a country of varied races and cultures. It was nationalistic, but deeply divided by sectional loyalties. It was in the "take-off" period of economic development—creating new industries, discovering new technologies, and experiencing booms and depressions.

During this quarter century, the American people made important decisions. They made them under conditions of stress and strain. On some vital questions, however, the American people remained indecisive. The generation of 1825–50 left a bitter problem for the next generation to resolve.

Physical Growth

Confusion and indecision were probably unavoidable. The physical growth of the nation alone placed great strains on its institutions. In 1820, the area of the states and territories of the Republic was 1,788,006 square miles; by mid-century, more than 1,200,000 additional square miles had been annexed to the country. In 1820 there were 24 states in the Union; by 1850, 30 states. In the same 30-year period, the population more than doubled; for every 100 Americans living in 1820, there were 241 living in 1850.

► Look at the maps on page C-6. What states joined the Union between 1820 and 1850? What new states were west of the Appalachian Mountains? West of the Mississippi River? What states depended for transportation on the Ohio, Missouri, and Mississippi river systems?

► Which two countries gave up their claims to Western lands between 1825 and 1850?

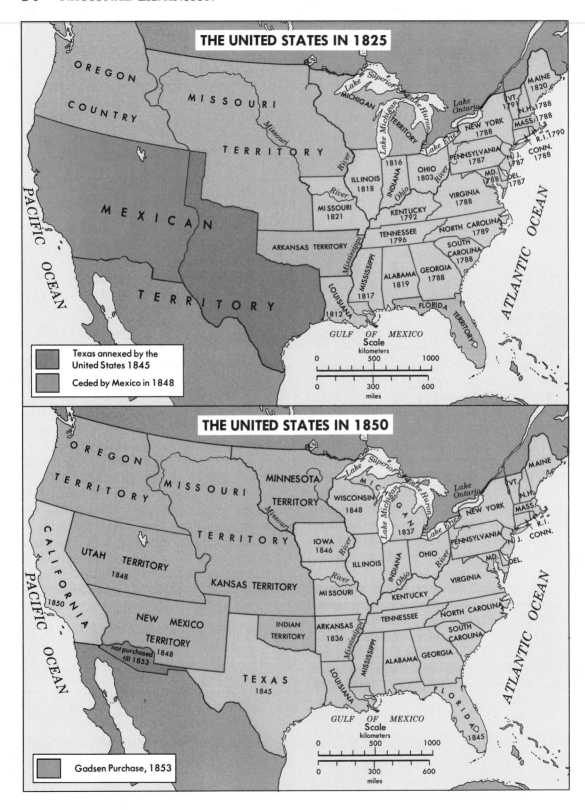

THE UNITED STATES IN 1825

THE UNITED STATES IN 1850

Immigration and Cultural Pluralism

In the year 1832 the number of immigrants jumped from about 22,000 a year to about 60,000. In the 1840's the annual entry rose still higher—to 100,000 and then 300,000. In the year 1850 nearly 370,000 foreigners arrived to settle in the United States. This flood of immigrants presented several challenges. How would such large numbers gain employment, shelter, and food?

Moreover, many immigrants brought customs which were strange to America. Many were Irish, driven from their homeland by a famine caused by a disease in the potato crop. These people were nearly all Roman Catholics. Many newcomers were Scandinavians and Germans. Some were German Jews. Thus new and varied cultural groups joined the existing patchwork of sectional, religious, and racial groups in the United States. How would the newcomers adjust to American ways? How would native Americans react to these large groups of foreigners?

● What friction might arise between the immigrants and the native groups?

Mexicans, Blacks, and Indians

Yet another ethnic group came into the Union when more Western territories were annexed. Many Spanish-speaking people lived in the areas from which the present states of Texas, New Mexico, Arizona, and California were created. The culture of these Mexicans and Mexican Indians differed from the cultural patterns in the East. However, except for some incidents in Texas, cultural conflicts between Hispanic and Anglo Americans were not obvious until after 1850.

Jefferson and other leaders of the early Republic had hoped that slavery would dwindle and die. They were wrong.

The black slave population grew steadily in the second quarter of the nineteenth century. In fact, the slave population more than doubled in the 30 years between 1820 and 1850. However, in the border slave states of Delaware and Maryland, slavery was dwindling. In these states free blacks outnumbered slaves by the time of the Civil War.

The lot of the free Negroes even outside the South was hampered by prejudice. Although conditions varied from one state to another, free blacks lived under many restrictions. They did not enjoy equal protection under law. Often they were denied the right to vote. Their education was neglected. Despite these disadvantages, black men and women of courage and talent emerged during this generation. One of the most important achievements of the black community during this period was the founding of a Negro press.

★ What is *prejudice?*
What is *cultural prejudice?*
What is *racial prejudice?*
What is *discrimination,* and how do cultural and racial prejudice lead to discrimination?

● Why did Negro slavery create racial prejudice even in free states?

The oldest native Americans also continued to suffer during this period. The peoples of the Southeast—Choctaw, Creek, Chickasaw, and Cherokee—were driven from their lands. Those who survived the long trek west settled in the area now called Oklahoma. The Seminole people of Florida were also attacked. Many of them, too, were driven west. The national government apparently meant to allow the Indians full possession of the area west of the Mississippi, but pioneers soon moved into these lands. Tribes that had hitherto known little or nothing of white men suffered the same sad history as Eastern Indians. Warfare and disease killed thousands. For example, the Mandan people on the Missouri River were wiped out by smallpox. Other peoples in the Northwest, such as the Nez Percé, accepted Christianity and adopted white men's farming methods. However, such attempts to adapt their cultures to new ways weakened the traditional institutions of the peoples. Wars broke out in the Oregon Country in the late 1840's. The stage was set for the final tragedy of the Plains Indians in the years after 1850.

● Why did Indian attempts to adopt white men's ways (*acculturation* or *assimilation*) so often lead to disaster for Indian peoples? Think of some of the problems that arise when a whole society tries to change its culture pattern in a hurry.

★ One result of culture shock and attempted acculturation may be *demoralization*. What does that mean? How does a *demoralized* person tend to behave?

● Why did white men and their governments so often break their treaties with Indians?

Immigrants landing from a ship

Swedish immigrants on their way to the West

Creating a Literary and Artistic Tradition

One achievement of the generation of 1825–50 was to establish an independent American intellectual tradition. Although Americans boasted of their new political institutions during the four decades after the Revolution, the United States could make no great display of achievements in literature, the arts, philosophy, and the sciences. In 1820 Sydney Smith, an eminent British wit and man of letters, wrote in the *Edinburgh Review* that as yet the United States had contributed little to civilization:

In the four quarters of the globe, who reads an American book? or goes to an American play? or looks at an American picture or statue? What does the world yet owe to American physicians or surgeons? What new substances have their chemists discovered? or what old ones have they analyzed? What new constellations have been discovered by the telescopes of Americans? What have they done in mathematics? Who drinks out of American glasses? or eats from American plates? or wears American coats and gowns? or sleeps in American blankets?

★   Before you read on, make sure you know the difference in meaning between *culture* in the broad sense used by anthropologists and sociologists, and culture in its more limited sense of intellectual and artistic activity. In these pages the phrase *intellectual culture* is used when reference is to the more limited type of culture.

(Left) Ralph W. Emerson

(Right) Frances E. W. Harper, an antislavery poet

Julia Ward Howe

Henry W. Longfellow

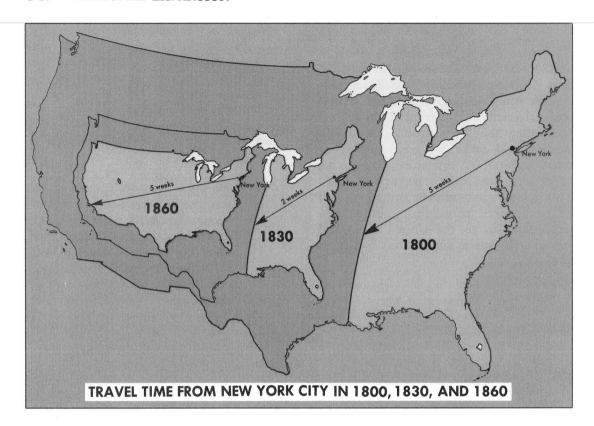

TRAVEL TIME FROM NEW YORK CITY IN 1800, 1830, AND 1860

Sidney Smith's sneers were justified in 1820. Yet by 1850 an American intellectual culture had emerged.

- Here are the names of writers some of whose works appeared between 1825 and 1850. Can you say what they were famous for? Washington Irving (1783–1859), James Fenimore Cooper (1789–1851), Ralph Waldo Emerson (1803–82), Edgar Allen Poe (1809–49), Herman Melville (1819–91), Henry Wadsworth Longfellow (1807–82), Francis Parkman (1823–93), William Hickling Prescott (1796–1859), John Greenleaf Whittier (1807–1892).

- How was American education likely to be affected by the rise of national intellectual culture? How would education be affected by the growth of industry and of cities?

Economic Development and Technological Improvements

The trend toward industrialization continued in the period 1825–50. Factories grew. Capital investment increased. The number of industrial workers multiplied.

- What social and economic problems does rapid industrialization bring?

The period also saw a number of American inventions. Some of these were vitally important in helping to open up new lands in the West. These included the reaper (or harvester), an improved steel-bladed plow, the Colt revolver, and the electric telegraph. Inventions that began to change industry and business during this period were the vulcanization of rubber, the sewing machine, and the rotary printing press.

In transportation, too, the generation of 1825–50 saw important advances. Canal building continued. So did the building of turnpikes. Perhaps the most important transportation improvement was the building of railroads. The first American railroad was opened in 1830. By 1850 the United States had more than 9,000 miles of railroad track.

- At the time of the Constitutional Convention, many Americans feared that the United States was too large to be governed by republican institutions. How did improved transportation and communication render such fears unfounded?

- Explain this generalization: "Human measurement of space and distance depends on the speed of travel and communication." Is this generalization borne out by recent history? Explain.

- How would *increased mobility* affect the lives of ordinary Americans?

DEMOCRACY IN AMERICA.

BY

ALEXIS DE TOCQUEVILLE.

TRANSLATED BY
HENRY REEVE, Esq.

A NEW EDITION,
WITH AN INTRODUCTORY NOTICE BY THE TRANSLATOR.

IN TWO VOLUMES.
VOL. I.

LONDON:
LONGMAN, GREEN, LONGMAN, AND ROBERTS.
1862.

(Above) Title page of a later edition of Tocqueville's famous book; (Right) Alexis de Tocqueville

The Challenge of Democracy

One of the three greatest challenges of 1825–50 was the spread of popular government. In 1800 the privilege of voting in 12 of the 15 states was limited to property owners. But by 1828 suffrage reforms brought a different concept of voting, and the number of voters was greatly increased; property requirements for the franchise began to vanish. Could the American political system remain free and just and orderly during this swift change? What would be the character of political leadership now that most men voted? Would America suffer from what Alexis de Tocqueville called the *tyranny of the majority?*

- What is meant by the expression *the tyranny of the majority?* How does the United States Constitution help protect citizens from this type of tyranny?

The 1830's and '40's revealed another fascinating democratic phenomenon.

This phenomenon was the rise of many kinds of *reform* movements. There were humanitarian movements, like antislavery, temperance, and prohibition (of alcoholic drinks). Prison reform, too, was in vogue. Other movements were directed to improving the status of women by giving them equal political rights with men and equal education. The problems of indus-trial society brought experiments in communistic living in settlements ranging from Massachusetts to Indiana. In some cases reform and experiment took religious forms, and new sects like the Latter-day Saints (Mormons) and Seventh-Day Adventists appeared. Reform Judaism came to America in the 1840's.

Some of these reform movements

(Top) A religious revival at a camp meeting in 1829
(Below) Robert Owen's new community at Harmony, Indiana

took the form of religious revivals following the pattern set by the Great Awakening a hundred years earlier. The great revival in upper New York State and Ohio was so enthusiastic that people spoke of certain areas as "burned-over." They meant that the fire of God's salvation had swept through the population. Not all the popular enthusiasms were innocent, however. The 1830's saw a number of violent and destructive riots directed against groups as varied as Catholics, Abolitionists, Freemasons, Mormons, and bankers. In frontier communities mob violence was often used to punish criminals or crush dissenting minorities.

(Top) The persecution and expulsion of the Mormons from Nauvoo, Illinois, September 18, 1846

(Below) A woodcut showing a proslavery riot in Alton, Illinois, on November 7, 1837

This cartoon makes fun of the expanded pretensions of the presidency under the rule of "King Andrew"

● Why might widespread popular participation in politics lead to many varied movements of social and moral reform? Why might it also lead to riots and violence? Does America today still have phenomena similar to those mentioned? Explain.

★ What is meant by *mass hysteria?* Should people avoid getting mixed up in a mob? Why?

★ Mob violence is not found only in democracies. There are many examples in the history of Europe in the Middle Ages and modern times. Some historians attribute mob violence in America to the lawlessness of the frontier. What is *vigilantism?* What is *lynch law?*[1]

Another phenomenon that seemed to be associated with democracy was the growing power of the president. In 1828 the election of the president became a nationwide popularity contest. Andrew Jackson saw himself as a popular leader, not merely the officer who executed the decisions of Congress. In part, this change grew out of the popular belief that government should respond to the will of the majority. The president was the only national official elected by a majority of nearly all the adult white males in the country. Jackson, therefore, considered himself the "tribune of the people"—their champion against special interests. For this reason, he vetoed more bills than had all preceding presidents combined, because he claimed that the bills were not in the public interest. Might the president grow too powerful?

● How might strengthening the executive branch of the federal government ease some of the strain of na-

---

[1]For a view of the violent aspects of American history, see Hugh Davis Graham and Ted Robert Gurr (eds.), *Violence in America: Historical and Comparative Perspective* (New York: Bantam Books, 1969). See especially Chapter 2, "Historical Patterns of Violence in America."

tional expansion? How might it cause additional difficulties? What might happen if large numbers of citizens should feel that a president represented sectional, rather than national, interests? May a popular leader turn into a dictator? Explain.

● A recurring problem in American history has been conflict between the president and the Congress. Each branch claims to represent the people, yet the two branches often disagree on policy. Why does this happen? What are the advantages and disadvantages of such conflicts?

● Most Latin American states have constitutions similar to that of the United States. Do these states also have conflicts between the executive and legislative branches? How are such conflicts resolved?

The coming of democracy and the changed role of the president once more revived the two-party system. In order to elect its candidate, a party had to aim at gaining a majority of the popular vote in as many states as possible. Would the new, powerful parties become tools of sectional interests and of ambitious, ruthless leaders? Would they encourage mob rule? Would parties dangerously divide the loyalties of the people? Or would a strong two-party system improve the checks and balances of the Constitution? Learning to live with parties was a major challenge of the period.

● The new parties called themselves Democrats and National Republicans (later Whigs). Why? What were the two parties of 1793 to 1815 called?

The Challenge of Imperialism

Popular emotions in politics found expression, too, in enthusiasm for expansionist policies. Many Americans were convinced that the United States must control the continent from the Atlantic to the Pacific and from the Rio Grande in the South to Oregon in the North. This policy of expansion came to be known as "manifest destiny." This phrase meant that the United States was obviously destined to rule the North American continent.

● What political obstacles would the United States meet in expanding west to the Pacific? In expanding south to the Rio Grande? In expanding northwest into the Oregon Country?

● What choices might be open to United States leaders in following manifest destiny? Negotiation? Purchase? Occupation by force? War? Explain.

● What might have happened in North America if the generation of 1825–50 had *not* insisted on imperialistic expansion?

● Andrew Jackson, president from 1829 to 1837, was a popular military hero from Tennessee. It has been said that the United States "needed" a westerner to lead it in these years.[2] Do you agree? Why or why not?

The Challenge of Sectionalism

The nation was by no means united in enthusiasm for manifest destiny. In fact, expansion was in many instances opposed by large blocs of popular opinion. This brings up the last and most difficult challenge of the period: the challenge of sectional division. This challenge was rendered more dangerous by the highly emotional moral problem of slavery.

---

[2]See *Alistair Cooke's America* (New York: Knopf, 1973), p. 166.

- Why did expansion—especially expansion southwest—intensify sectional hostility? Recall the Missouri Compromise.
- What is *political loyalty*, or *allegiance*? How might the political loyalties of Americans be divided and uncertain as a result of imperialistic policies, sectionalism, the slavery issue, and the two-party system? Might a situation arise in which other loyalties might replace loyalty to the Union? Explain. What loyalties might take precedence in different persons over loyalty to the nation?

Conflicting Loyalties 1825-50

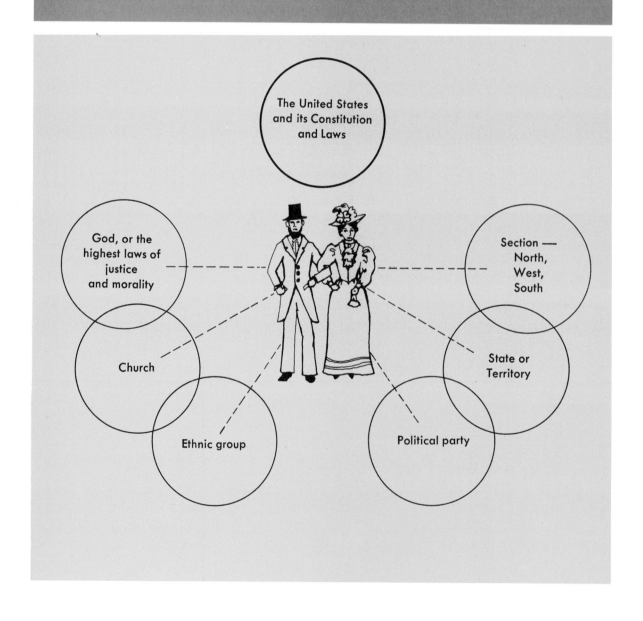

Dilemmas

The generation of 1825–50 must have grown increasingly nervous and insecure as sectional tensions became more acute. By 1850 manifest destiny had been fulfilled, though some thought it still beckoned toward Cuba. But manifest destiny had intensified, not lessened, sectional hostilities. As for democracy: it was working, but how long would it continue to work? How long could decisions about the future of slavery be put off? Decisive in some things, but dangerously indecisive in others: that was the character of the generation of 1825–50.

Wagons moving west along the Santa Fe Trail

President John Quincy Adams

President Andrew Jackson

1

A New Era in Politics

The Era of Good Feelings Ends

When John Quincy Adams was chosen president in 1825, the "Era of Good Feelings" died. By the end of Adams's administration, America's practical politics looked very different from the politics of the Federalists and the Virginia dynasty. Long later, such American writers as Henry Adams and T. S. Eliot said that in the United States *dignified* politics came to an end with the defeat of J. Q. Adams in 1828.

By 1815 the Federalist party had ceased to be a national political organization; within a few years it was extinct. In 1824 and 1825, most of the leading men in America belonged to the Democratic-Republican party, which claimed to inherit the principles of Thomas Jefferson. Soon, however, the Democratic-Republican party was tormented by clashing interests within its ranks. Like the Federalist party before it, the Democratic-Republican party was falling apart.

► What acts or attitudes of the Federalist party destroyed its effectiveness as a national political party?

● How might the absence of an opposing party cause divisions within a party to become more serious?

In 1820 there had been only one serious candidate for the office of president — James Monroe, the incumbent. It had not even been necessary to nominate him formally. Until 1820 *congressional caucuses*, informal meetings of party members who held seats in Congress, chose presidential candidates. But now "King Caucus" was dying. Caucuses could be dominated easily by a small number of congressional politicians. People felt that this concentration of power was "undemocratic." Here is how the caucus system worked — or failed to work — in 1824.

Fewer than one-third of the Democratic-Republican party's congressional members attended the 1824 caucus. The caucus nominated for the presidency William H. Crawford, of Georgia, Monroe's secretary of the treasury — a leader of the old planter aristocracy. Crawford was also nominated by Virginia's legislature. However, three other presidential candidates were nominated in 1824 — nominated not by the caucus, but by state legislatures or mass meetings. One was John Quincy Adams of Massachusetts, son of President John Adams; he was New England's candidate. Another was Andrew Jackson, a military hero then in the Senate; he came from Tennessee and was a spokesman for the West. The fourth candidate was Henry Clay of Kentucky, Speaker of the House — also standing for the West.

★ How are presidential candidates nominated today?

● Critics complained that the caucus system ignored the principle of separation of powers. In what way is this true? How might the caucus system give Congress excessive control over the executive branch of the federal government?

★ Find the probable origin of the word *caucus*. Use a good dictionary.

So the election of fall 1824 turned into a brawl. In the midst of the campaign, Secretary Crawford suffered a paralyzing stroke. Even though it seemed improbable that he could recover sufficiently to serve as president, his supporters would not withdraw his name. John Quincy Adams, the candidate with the most impressive accomplishments, was hampered by his cold personality. Henry Clay's personality won

him friends, but his position in the House of Representatives had made enemies for him. Jackson, a successful general, had shown little legislative or diplomatic skill.

★ Look up biographical information about these four candidates. Write a campaign speech for one of them: try to emphasize points that would most appeal to the American voters of that era.

Of the candidates, only Henry Clay brought forth a detailed program for national action. His *American System* promised prosperity and rapid growth to the country. In this campaign, however, issues did not play so important a part as did personalities and sectional interests. When the voting took place, no candidate won a majority in the electoral college.

According to the Twelfth Amendment to the Constitution of the United

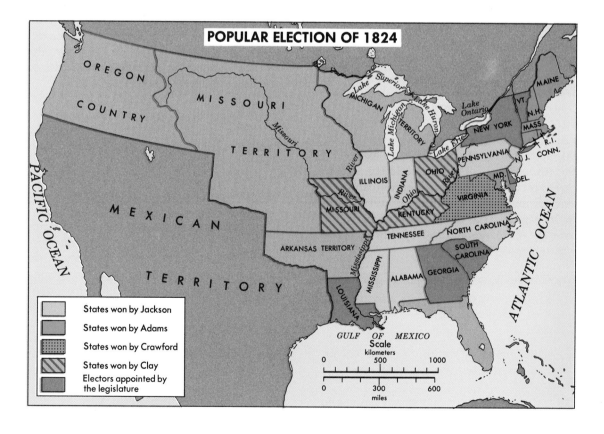

POPULAR ELECTION OF 1824

States won by Jackson
States won by Adams
States won by Crawford
States won by Clay
Electors appointed by the legislature

The Presidential Election, 1824

Candidate	Home State	Popular Vote	Number of electoral votes	States
Jackson	Tennessee	108,740 (30.5%)	99	11
Adams	Massachusetts	153,544 (43.1%)	84	7
Crawford	Georgia	46,618 (13.2%)	41	3
Clay	Kentucky	47,136 (13.2%)	37	3
			261	

(needed to win, 131)

States, if no presidential candidate receives a clear majority in the electoral college, the president must be chosen by the House of Representatives. The House must choose from the three candidates having the most votes. This situation now occurred for the first time in the history of the American Republic.

★ Make sure you know the difference between a *clear majority* and a *relative majority* (or *plurality*). Which type of majority did Jackson win in the electoral college in 1824?

★ Look up Amendment XII to the Constitution.

● Look at the table showing election results in 1824. Which candidate would have to withdraw from the final balloting in the House of Representatives? Which, by reason of his office, might exercise special influence in the House ballot?

● Which candidate—Adams or Jackson—might expect to be supported by Henry Clay? Why?

Once the results of the 1824 election in the several states became known, Henry Clay was courted by the other three candidates. Although he could not be chosen president, he probably could decide who would be elected. "King-Maker" Clay began to weigh his decision.

Jackson, like Clay, represented the Western section. However, Jackson did not approve of Clay's American System, since it involved using the national government's power (and money) for improvements in transportation. On the other hand, although Adams and Clay were so different in personality, they had similar ideas for America's growth. Clay went to work on the members of the House of Representatives. John Quincy Adams was chosen the sixth president of the United States, early in 1825, by the House of Representatives.

Jackson and his many supporters came to believe that they had been cheated. They claimed (almost certainly wrongly) that Adams made a secret deal with Clay. The deal was, supposedly, to make Clay secretary of state. That is what John Quincy Adams actually did soon after becoming president.

● Later, Clay said that he felt that he made a mistake in accepting the sec-

Henry Clay of Kentucky. A leader of the War Hawks in the War of 1812. The Great Compromiser

retaryship. Can you see why? How did the action harm Adams and Clay politically?

- How did the disputed election of 1824–25 lead to political bitterness? How did it bring the Era of Good Feelings to a sharp close?

President John Quincy Adams and His Plans

Adams had been an efficient secretary of state. Somewhat cold in manner, and never sparing of himself or others, Adams held a low opinion of most men. The harshness of his language had offended many, at home and abroad. Yet he had formed a strong American foreign policy, especially where Latin America was concerned. The "Monroe Doctrine" was Adams's achievement. Always in favor of vigorous action by the United States, Adams had advocated expansion of his country in instance after instance. When

General Jackson had conquered Florida from the Spaniards (in the First Seminole War), Adams had been the only member of the cabinet to support Jackson. In 1819 he induced Spain to accept America's claims to lands northwest of Texas as far as the Pacific.

Adams thought it natural enough that he should become president, as his father had been before him, and he had elaborate plans for improving the United States. Although Congress did not accept his plans, the nation was prosperous, secure, and well governed during his presidency.

Yet good government is not necessarily popular government. From the first, the younger Adams failed to please most of the people of the United States. For one thing, Andrew Jackson's friends continued to claim that the appointment of Clay as secretary of state was a corrupt bargain. Detractors said that Adams was a hypocrite—a Puritan in manner, but a conniving politician at heart. His New England heritage did, indeed, damage Adams's popularity. His reserve, his self-righteousness, and his chilly manner did not warm men's hearts. Adams was the best educated man in public life, but the majority of the people did not relish being governed by a professor. Adams was too proud, and too honest, to beg for public approval.

Adams meant to make the United States great — but not through mere recklessness and thoughtless growth. Adams believed that the course of American public policy should be planned well in advance. Science and industry must be systematically promoted. A new system of uniform weights and measures must be adopted. The national government should develop the economy through the construction of a vast network of roads and canals. The public lands should be kept as a treasure, to benefit future generations by gradual development. The whole world, he hoped, might be persuaded to follow America's example. Then freedom and justice might triumph everywhere.

★ Adams's plans for the United States may remind you of discussions nowadays about America's environment or ecology. If Adams had succeeded in persuading Congress and the people to approve his plans, how might the United States today be different?

● Who would oppose Adams's plans for a network of highways and canals at national expense? Who would oppose his plans for protective tariffs, and why?

Public opinion was not moving in Adams's direction. In the South and the West, many people resented the increasing power of the national government, and were listening to Representative John Randolph's warnings that if central government could confer benefits, it might also

The Growth of Tariffs 1816-28

1816	Duty of 25% on woolen, cotton, and iron manufactures; 30% on paper, leather, hats; 15% on all other goods
1818	Some rates increased
1824	Increased duties on iron, lead, glass, hemp; 33⅓% on cotton and woolen manufactures; 15% on raw wool
1828	Duty of 50% plus 4 cents per pound on raw wool; 45% on most woolens; increased duties on iron; $60 a ton on hemp; duty of 10 cents a gallon on molasses (The Tariff of Abominations was so complicated that it cannot really be summarized here!)

work harm. High tariffs were bitterly disliked by those who would have to pay higher prices, but who received no immediate benefits. All along the frontier, men hungered for more land, and cursed Adams for not making it easily available to them. Besides, they thought Adams was too kind to the Indians. Most of all, perhaps, the American public in those years objected to being told what was good for them. Thus the Adams program was so unacceptable to the mass of people that even Adams's friends in Congress dared not try to enact it.

The Tariff of Abominations

In the matter of the tariff, J. Q. Adams did not act strongly enough. Though he recommended a protective tariff, he did not specify the rates or say just how protective this tax on imports should be. Everything was left to Congress. And Congress, after much partisan haggling,

A poster for the election of Andrew Jackson in 1828

adopted the *Tariff of Abominations* — with rates so high and so unjust that some members of Congress who voted for the bill were astonished that it passed. All sorts of people were enraged. In fact, the whole affair had been arranged by the supporters of Andrew Jackson, so that the voters would blame Adams for this unfair legislation.[1] Although Adams said Congress was responsible, he signed the bill — and the public did blame him.

★ President Adams ought to have vetoed the tariff for political reasons, and because it was truly a mixture of abominations. However, he — like earlier presidents — thought the veto was intended to be used only against *unconstitutional* laws. Find out which president started the *political* use of the veto. Why might Adams have felt that such political use violated the separation of powers?

---

[1] See Edward Channing, *A History of the United States*, Vol. V (New York: Macmillan, 1927), pp. 371–72, and George Dangerfield *The Era of Good Feelings* (New York: Harcourt, Brace and World, Harbinger Books, 1963), pp. 399–409.

★ What can you learn about political maneuvering from the history of the Tariff of Abominations? Do similar machinations still occur? Why cannot the voters "see through" such maneuvers? How does the separation of powers encourage such activities? Could a British prime minister be similarly outmaneuvered by enemies in Parliament? Why or why not?

● What are the arguments in favor of protective tariffs? What are the arguments against them? How does the Tariff of Abominations illustrate one of the big objections to tariffs?

A New Sort of Presidential Election

The Tariff of Abominations was passed in 1828, just in time to add fuel to the flames of party struggle in the presidential election. This election was different in many ways from earlier ones. Before 1828, presidential elections were usually relatively tame. National political parties were not well organized, and the

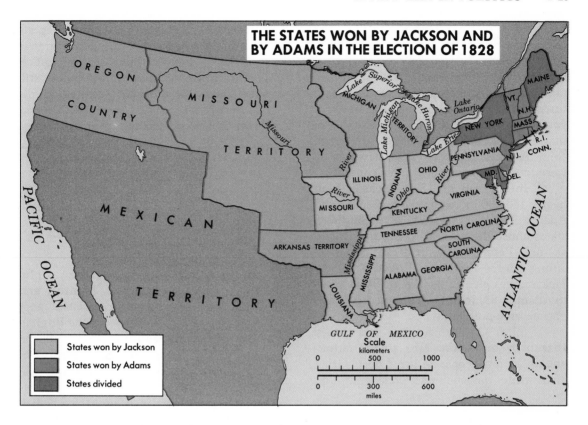

THE STATES WON BY JACKSON AND BY ADAMS IN THE ELECTION OF 1828

Scale
kilometers
0   500   1000

0   300   600
miles

- States won by Jackson
- States won by Adams
- States divided

large majority of citizens did not vote. But pressures for a change had been accumulating, and these pressures burst the old framework of politics in 1828, when Andrew Jackson ran against John Quincy Adams for the presidency.

One important change was in the method of choosing presidential electors. The Constitution allowed every state to decide for itself the method of selecting its electors. In the earlier years of the Republic, state legislatures chose the electoral college. But by 1828, only Delaware and South Carolina followed the old practice. In all the other states, presidential electors were chosen directly by the voters.

Another major change was the extension of the suffrage. From colonial times, the right to vote had been associated with the holding of property—especially of land. It was argued that landholders had a "special stake" in society, and that only they could be trusted to make prudent

judgments. In the colonial years, and in the earlier years of the Republic, this restriction was not harsh. Most Americans lived on farms, and even the majority of townspeople possessed "freeholds" valuable enough to qualify them for voting.

As time passed, the growth of big towns had changed this situation. The class of landless city dwellers grew. The new Western states, where democratic ideas flourished, opened the franchise to all adult white males as soon as they were admitted to statehood. Consequently, the Eastern states relaxed their voting requirements. By 1828 landowning was no longer an important consideration in the exercise of the vote in nearly all states. This meant that many more people were entitled to vote in 1828 than had been in 1824. In Pennsylvania, for instance, there had been only 47,000 voters in the presidential election of 1824. There were 150,000 voters in that state in the election of 1828.

Most of these new voters preferred the "democratic" Jackson to the "aristocratic" Adams. Andrew Jackson's political machine was efficient. Parades, songs, mass barbecues, and fighting speeches captured the interest of the voters. Newspapers were more active in this campaign than they had been since the presidency of John Adams. Eighteen new newspapers were founded to back Jackson's candidacy.

In the fall of 1828, Jackson won nearly 180,000 more popular votes than did Adams. All the Western and Southern states chose the general by big majorities, as did Pennsylvania. Adams remained strong only in New England. Thus Jackson was elected by 178 electoral votes to Adams's 83. John C. Calhoun again was chosen vice-president.

John Quincy Adams was badly shaken by his defeat. His famous father, one of the few people he loved deeply, had died while the son was president. The younger Adams, who now was 62 years old, seemed exhausted by the mountains of work that he had attempted while in office. Yet there was a courageous future still before him: he was soon elected to the House of Representatives, and became Congress's foremost opponent of slavery.

★ Has any other former president held important political office after leaving the White House? Why did not J. Q. Adams run for the presidency again?

A Democratic Autocrat in Power

Presidents Washington, John Adams, Jefferson, Madison, Monroe, and John Quincy Adams were polished gentlemen, formed more or less on the English model, thoroughly educated, and (with the partial exception of Jefferson) dignified in their manners. President Jackson was distinctly unlike his predecessors. His upbringing had been radically different, for he had been a poor immigrant's son, and had led a rough, poverty-stricken life as a boy.

He fought in the Revolution as a boy private. He studied law rather carelessly, then settled in Tennessee and was elected as that new state's only member of the House of Representatives. For a time he was a justice of the Tennessee Supreme Court, and later became a planter. He killed a man in a duel, and was badly wounded in another duel. As a general of volunteers, he smashed the Creek Indians, and won Florida from Spain. He defeated the British at New Orleans in 1815. He then was the first governor of Florida Territory; after which he was elected senator from Tennessee in 1823. Clearly he was a man of great energy, but it remained to be seen whether he could be a competent president.

Kitchen Cabinet and Spoils System

The men whom Jackson chose for his cabinet were not impressive. Only one,

Andrew Jackson before he became president

Martin Van Buren, was well known. Soon it was said that Jackson was guided by a *Kitchen Cabinet* of friends with little talent and few scruples. Believing that a new broom should sweep clean, President Jackson removed about 2,000 experienced officeholders and replaced them with new men faithful to himself.

Some of the people he wanted to appoint were so clearly incompetent that the Senate, despite Jackson's popularity, refused to confirm a good many of his nominations for posts in the federal government. Although Jackson did not originate the *spoils system* — that is, using public appointments to reward one's political henchmen — he introduced it as a regular feature of American politics.

★ Why is the system called the *spoils system?* The polite name for it was *rotation in office.* What does that mean?

★ In eighteenth-century Britain, *patronage* was used by the government as a way of "managing" Parliament. Did this differ from the spoils system? How?

● Look at the box with quotations from Emerson and Jackson on the spoils system. What are the strong points of the system? What are its weaknesses? If you were president would you favor it? Why or why not?

★ How does our civil service system today differ from the spoils system? Do any offices change hands when a new president takes office?

Political Battle Lines

The spoils system was a sign that democratic notions were predominant. Another result of democratic ideas was the new role of the president. Jackson felt himself called upon to use his office to fight Congress and the "special interests" that Congress represented.

Another strong man, however, presided over the Senate of the United States. He was John C. Calhoun, of South Carolina, the "Cast-Iron Man," as tough in his way as was Jackson, "Old Hickory." Once upon a time, Calhoun had been a nationalist and a "war hawk." But as circumstances changed, and as Calhoun was influenced by the arguments of Senator John Randolph against central power, the vice-president became a champion of state powers and Southern interests.

● Both J. Q. Adams and Calhoun were enthusiastic nationalists when Monroe was president. Both hoped and expected that the United States would expand west and south. Yet in the 1830's they became sectional leaders, who helped to divide the na-

Two Views of the Spoils System

Ralph Waldo Emerson wrote:

What an excellent principle our favorite rule of rotation in office would be if applied to industrial matters. You have been watchmaker long enough, now it is my turn to make watches, and you can bake muffins. The carpenter is to make glass this year, and the glassblower staircases. The blacksmith is to cut me a coat, and the tailor is to take charge of the machine-shop.

Andrew Jackson said:

The duties of all public officers are, or at least admit of being made, so plain and simple that men of intelligence may readily qualify themselves for their performance. And I cannot but believe that more is lost by the long continuance of men in office than is generally to be gained by their experience. . . . In a country where offices are created solely for the benefit of the people, no one man has any more right to official station than another.

tion. Calhoun encouraged expansion. Adams opposed expansion bitterly. Can you explain the great change in the attitudes of the two statesmen?

Calhoun had allied himself with Jackson for some years, but now a coolness arose between them. It was rumored that Jackson would not support Calhoun for re-election, but would prefer Van Buren as vice-president. Some sly politicians informed the president that in 1818 Calhoun had desired to censure Jackson for his behavior during the conquest of Florida—which the president had not guessed before. This caused a break between president and vice-president. Calhoun's friends were pushed out of the Jackson cabinet, and it became clear that Jackson meant to put Van Buren into Calhoun's place at the end of 1832. The lines were drawn for a fierce struggle between the Westerner and the Southerner.

About the same time, Jackson began to come into conflict with Northern and Eastern financial groups. These groups supported the Bank of the United States and a national system of expanding credit. Jackson's party supported state banks and hated the Bank of the United States. On the whole, Jackson's attitude was widely popular in the states of the Western and Middle sections.

The Fight Against Calhoun and South Carolina over Nullification

It was not the debate about slavery that nearly split the Union between 1830 and 1833, for both Jackson and Calhoun were slaveholders. It was the rate of taxes on imports (tariffs) that nearly brought armed conflict between the national power and a state government.

South Carolina, like the other Southern states, depended on cash crops, the larger part of which were sold abroad.

In return, Southerners bought many manufactured goods from abroad. Britain especially was a major importer of raw cotton, and a major exporter of manufactures—including cotton and woolen textiles. The New England and Middle Atlantic states, however, increasingly depended on manufacturing rather than agriculture. The leading men of those states desired to build up American industry by a system of protective tariffs, or high rates of duty upon imports. The tariffs would make imported goods expensive. Thus, American customers would buy American manufactures rather than imported goods.

However profitable such a policy might be to the North, it harmed the South, which needed to import inexpensive cloth and other manufactures from Europe. Southerners especially objected to the Tariff of Abominations of 1828. This tariff set extremely high tariffs on many goods, both manufactures and raw materials. The South got nothing from the tariff except higher costs of living. Meanwhile the prices of cotton and other Southern crops fell.

● Look at the simple graph on page C-29. What happens to the standard of living of producers of cash crops like cotton when the price of manufactures soars and the price of crops sinks?

South Carolina was hardest hit by the crisis. Most citizens of that state believed the Tariff of Abominations to be discriminatory and unconstitutional. They looked to the vice-president, John Caldwell Calhoun, their own chief statesman, to save them from the effects of the tariff. What could be done? In cooperation with other South Carolina leaders, Calhoun developed the doctrine of *nullification*. If the Congress should enact unjust legislation, Calhoun and his colleagues argued, the effective remedy was for a state to nullify (refuse to obey) such unjust laws. If necessary, the state should withdraw from the Union.

★ Had threats of nullification or secession been made before this time? How did Jefferson lead the protest against the Alien and Sedition Acts? What did many New England leaders suggest in connection with the War of 1812?

● Behind threats of nullification and secession lay a deep division over the interpretation of the Constitution of the United States. That division remained until the issue was settled by civil war. Look at the box, "The Webster-Hayne Debate." Which argument seems more valid? Why? Do you think that the Constitution was unclear on this matter? How *was* the Constitution ratified? By the whole people? Or by state conventions?

★ What distant echoes of the arguments of American colonists in favor of independence from Britain can be detected in the argument for nullification and secession?

★ Make sure you know what is meant by *strict construction, broad construction, sovereign,* and *compact.*

Popular opinion in South Carolina was behind Calhoun and Hayne. Van Buren and other members of the Jackson administration urged the president to warn South Carolina of the consequences before that state should secede. At a banquet hon-

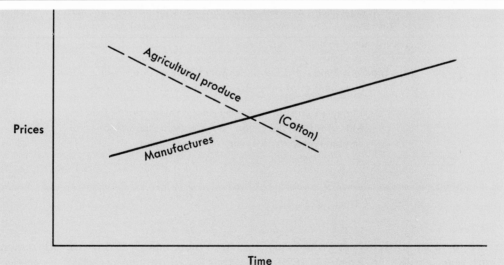

The Classic Scissors Crisis that Farmers have often faced. Southern planters faced it in 1829-32.

This type of graph is called a "scissors." Can you see why? Who is likely to be cut by the scissors? People engaged in manufacture? or people engaged in agriculture (cotton growing)?

The Webster — Hayne Debate

In January 1830, two senators debated the topic of nullification. *Robert Y. Hayne* of South Carolina expressed the view of the Constitution developed by Calhoun.

Hayne's main points were:

1. The Constitution must be strictly, not broadly, construed.

2. A strict construction shows that states' rights are superior to the authority of the national government when the national government extends its powers unconstitutionally.

3. The Constitution was and remains a compact between sovereign states.

   Therefore states retain the right to interpose their power to nullify unjust acts by the national government, and even to separate themselves from the Union.

Daniel Webster of Massachusetts replied:

1. The states are not sovereign in areas where the Constitution grants powers to the national government.

2. A disagreement between states and national government must be settled by the federal courts, or a constitutional amendment, or regular elections.

3. The Constitution was not a compact between states, but a popular government established by the will of the whole people.

   Therefore no state can nullify national laws or legally withdraw from the Union. Such actions are treason, and can only result in civil war.

oring the memory of Jefferson (who had died four years earlier) on April 13, 1830, President Jackson arose to propose a toast. Staring at Vice-President Calhoun, he exclaimed loudly, "Our Union! It must be preserved!" Calhoun replied with another toast: "The Union! Next to our liberty most dear!" The vice-president paused, and then added, "May we all remember that it can only be preserved by respecting the rights of the Union."

The challenge had been offered and accepted. By July, President Jackson was suggesting that if South Carolina should nullify federal laws, force must be used to keep that state in the Union. He told a

South Carolina congressman that "If one drop of blood be shed there in defiance of the laws of the United States, I will hang the first man of them I can get my hands on to the first tree I can find."

By the middle of the summer of 1831, Calhoun openly supported the nullifiers. The new tariff act of 1832 somewhat altered taxes upon imports, but did not satisfy the Southerners. In December 1832, a state convention in South Carolina formally nullified the tariff acts of 1828 and 1832. Those measures were declared "null, void, and no law"—not binding upon South Carolina. People began to talk of Calhoun as the future "first president of the Southern Confederacy." Already President Jackson was gathering troops and naval vessels to subdue South Carolina by force, if need be. "General Dale," he told a friend, "if this thing goes on, our country will be like a bag of meal with both ends open. Pick it up in the middle or endwise, and it will run out. I must tie the bag and save the country."

Old Hickory was ready to fight once more. He asked Congress to pass a "Force Bill," authorizing him to move against South Carolina. No other state offered to assist South Carolina. Yet that state would not yield to Jackson's demands that it obey Congress. As February 1, 1833, approached, Van Buren and other politicans from several states feared that the Union would be torn apart. Who could prevent shots being fired?

They turned to Senator Henry Clay, the master of compromise and conciliation. On February 12, Clay introduced in Congress a new tariff schedule, providing for the gradual abandoning of all import taxes amounting to more than 20 per cent of the value of the imports. This satisfied South Carolina and the other Southern states fairly well. South Carolina gave up its nullification of the tariff, and Jackson did not resort to arms.

● If fighting had broken out between South Carolina and the federal gov-

From this wharf in Charleston, South Carolina, cotton was shipped to ports at home and abroad

Nicholas Biddle

ernment in 1833, what states might have aided South Carolina? Why was there less support then for South Carolina than in 1861?

★ Does the Preamble to the Constitution of the United States imply that the "people" of the whole country, together, have made a "more perfect union"? Or does it mean that the people of the several states, taken separately, have made this union? What legal and historical arguments can be advanced on either side?

The Fight with Biddle and the Bank: Phase One, 1831–32

When the nullification struggle was on, Jackson had another fight on his hands. He was determined to destroy the Bank of the United States. The president of the Bank was Nicholas Biddle of Phila-

delphia. Biddle represented the financial and business interests of the Northeastern and Middle states.

★ The Bank of the United States had been abolished once before. When and why? What were Jefferson's views on the first Bank of the United States?

● Why was Jackson opposed to the Bank? What sections or groups in the United States wanted the Bank destroyed?

★ What had the Supreme Court decided about the Bank in *McCulloch* v. *Maryland*, 1819?

Chartered by the national government in 1816, the second Bank of the United States was a private corporation which kept on deposit the funds that the federal government collected in taxes. The Bank's friends intended this national financial institution to build up the nation's credit, to the profit both of the country and of the Bank's stockholders. Its popularity in the North was counterbalanced by suspicion of the Bank, as a monopoly, in the South and in the West.

Although Andrew Jackson knew little of finance, he was suspicious of banks generally, and of the United States Bank in particular. Many banks had failed during his lifetime. Was the Bank of the United States truly sound? And might it not become an octopus, its tentacles reaching into every state, controlling the nation's economy? He thought that the directors of the Bank had opposed his election in 1828. Was it not all too possible that the Bank might intervene cleverly in politics? Jackson was sure that the Bank tried to manipulate Congress. Moreover, Jackson believed, as Jefferson had believed, that the Bank was *unconstitutional*.

Such reasoning persuaded Jackson that the Bank must be destroyed. The majority in Congress did not share the president's distrust of the United States Bank. Nicholas Biddle, an experienced lawyer and diplomat, would be difficult to defeat. Yet Jackson determined to fight the Bank as relentlessly as he had fought the British at New Orleans. It was clear that the Bank would be a principal issue in the presidential campaign of 1832, although the Bank's charter would not expire until 1836.

Nicholas Biddle, backed by Senators Webster, Clay, and others, decided to ask Congress for a new Bank charter, in defiance of Jackson. Biddle believed that this boldness would be admired by most Americans. The Senate and the House approved the Bank's new charter, in the summer of 1832. As he had promised, President Jackson vetoed the Bank bill. Led by their presidential candidate, Henry Clay, the National Republicans made defense of the Bank the principal theme of their campaign in that year's election. The Democrats rallied behind Jackson, who attacked the Bank in nearly every speech he made. The majority of Americans must have approved of Jackson's attacks, for the election gave Jackson 219 electoral votes and Clay only 49.

- Look at the table on page C-34. Where was Jackson's main support? Would you expect New York and Pennsylvania to vote against the Bank? What does their vote suggest about the attitude of ordinary men and women toward the business and financial groups?

- Notice the relation between the popular vote and the electoral vote. Why is the electoral vote generally greatly exaggerated compared with the popular vote? Do you think this exaggeration is desirable? Why or why not?

★ What is a third party? Can you name any later or present-day third parties?

★ Find out more about the Anti-Masonic party. How does this party illustrate the tendency of democratic politics to produce special reform groups or special interest groups?

● The opponents of the Bank had very mixed motives. One set of opponents, including Jackson himself, distrusted credit and easy money; they wanted *hard money* (gold and silver coinage or notes exchangeable for gold). The other group wanted even *easier money* than the Bank of the United States allowed; they wanted state and local banks that would provide easy credit for farmers for buying land. What do you think of this alliance against the Bank? Might the abolition of the national bank help bring on an economic crisis and panic? Explain.

The Bank Fight: Phase Two, 1833–36

Jackson had four more years in the White House—sufficient time to put an end to the Bank. Still Biddle and the other officers of the Bank believed that Jackson could not crush their institution. If the national government should withdraw its deposits from their vaults, they argued, the Bank would have to call in its loans; and what is now called a "depression" would result. When the people felt the practical effects of Jackson's policy, they would protest.

Knowing that a sudden withdrawal of federal deposits would indeed injure commerce and manufacturing, Jackson drew up a plan for reducing those deposits gradually. By degrees, his new secretary of the treasury, Roger Taney (later Chief Justice of the United States), transferred governmental funds from the United States Bank to 23 state banks. From October 1, 1833, onward, the United States Bank shriveled. In the Senate, Clay, Webster, and Calhoun thundered against Jackson's

The Presidential Election, 1832

Candidates	Party	Popular Vote	Electoral Vote
Andrew Jackson	Democratic	687,502 (55.0%)	219
Henry Clay	National Republican	530,189 (42.4%)	49
William Wirt	Anti-Masonic		7
John Floyd	National Republican	33,108 (2.6%)	11

How the States Went

Jackson carried 16⅓ states:

> In New England: Maine and New Hampshire
> In the Middle Section: New York, Pennsylvania, and New Jersey
> In the Seaboard South: Virginia, North Carolina, Georgia, and part of Maryland
> In the Southwest: Alabama, Mississippi, Louisiana, Tennessee
> In the West: Missouri, Ohio, Indiana, Illinois

Clay carried 5⅔ states: Massachusetts, Connecticut, Rhode Island, Delaware, Kentucky, and part of Maryland

Wirt, who represented a third party with a special aim,* carried Vermont

Floyd was chosen by the South Carolina legislature

*The Anti-Masonic party opposed the Freemasons and other secret societies. It was the first "third party" in our history.

policy. Congress formally *censured* Jackson for his destruction of the Bank.

This unprecedented action by Congress could not restore the Bank's power and prosperity. By the beginning of 1837, Jackson had triumphed even in Congress. Never again did the national government authorize a national bank as the depository of the government's entire revenues.

For ten years after Jackson defeated Biddle and the Bank, the United States had no central banking system at all. Not until 1846 was an independent Treasury of the United States established—a measure which has lasted, though modified and improved, to our own time.

★ Why was it thought necessary, before Jackson's time, to charter a national bank? Why does the national government need an elaborate national apparatus for making large loans? How can the United States manage without an official national bank today? Do most countries have their own national banks now? Is there in America some financial

A cartoon of Jackson's opposition to the bank

apparatus today that fulfills many of the functions of the old Bank of the United States?

★ What is a *censure* by Congress? Has any president been censured in recent years?

● Soon after the Bank lost its charter and deposits, a severe economic crisis occurred. Many state banks became bankrupt. The price of cotton fell 50 per cent. There was widespread unemployment. The depression lasted until 1842–43. Do you think the ending of the Bank encouraged the depression? Explain.

★ The crisis and panic were also encouraged by Jackson's *hard money* policy. Find out about the *Specie Circular* and its effects. Why did Jackson feel it necessary to issue the circular?

Political Alliances: The Jacksonian Coalition

Students of American politics have discovered that victory in national elections usually depends on an alliance of differing interests. The successful political leader is a person who can put together an *alliance*, or *coalition*, of groups. One group may want one thing (like higher prices for farm products), another group may want something quite different (like higher wages for industrial workers), and still another may want something else (like financial help for older, retired people). The art of the political leader, will be to do *something* to satisfy each group. If he does the job well, he may create a coalition that will give a winning majority across the nation for 20 years or more.

● A political alliance may be hard to hold together. Look at the examples in the preceding paragraph. How might the basic interests of the three groups contradict one another?

● Should a political leader try to put into effect policies other than those designed to please the groups in his coalition? Explain.

The political party organized by the Jackson men was a coalition. Factions within the party represented different interests. In Pennsylvania, industrial interests were powerful; so Pennsylvanian Democrats worked for protective tariffs. Democrats in agricultural and commercial South Carolina, on the other hand, favored free trade. Western Democrats desired improvements like roads and canals at federal expense. New York Democrats believed that such projects should be the responsibility

The Presidential Election of 1836

Candidates	Party	Popular Vote	Electoral Vote
Martin Van Buren	Democratic	761,549 (50.9%)	170
William Harrison	Whig	549,567 (36.7%)	73
Hugh L. White	Whig	145,396 (9.7%)	26
Daniel Webster	Whig	41,287 (2.7%)	14

How the States Went

Two new states had joined since 1832: Arkansas and Michigan. Thus 26 states took part in the election.

Van Buren's States (15):

> In New England: Maine, New Hampshire, Rhode Island, Connecticut
> In the Middle Section: New York and Pennsylvania
> In the Seaboard South: Virginia, North Carolina
> In the Western South: Alabama, Mississippi, Louisiana, Arkansas
> In the Midwest: Illinois, Missouri, Michigan

Harrison's States (7):

> Vermont, New Jersey, Delaware, Maryland, Ohio, Kentucky, Indiana

Webster took only Massachusetts

White took Georgia and Tennessee

South Carolina once again chose its own candidate, William P. Mangum

> Note that the Whig party was split between three *sectional* candidates: Webster (Massachusetts), White (Tennessee), Harrison (Ohio). The Whigs hoped this would throw the election into the House of Representatives.

The Presidential Election, 1840

Candidates	Party	Popular Vote	Electoral Vote
William H. Harrison	Whig	1,275,017 (53.1%)	234
Martin Van Buren	Democratic	1,128,702 (46.9%)	60

How the States Went

Van Buren won only 7 states: New Hampshire, Virginia, South Carolina, Alabama, Arkansas, Missouri, Illinois

Harrison took the remaining 19 states

of individual states. Some influential Southern Democrats looked upon Jackson as a friend to state sovereignty and a leader who would not be influenced by Abolitionists.

By 1836, the other major party, which took the name of "Whig," also represented a coalition of interests. But the range of opinions among the Whigs was narrower, and the party's programs were more consistent. Henry Clay was the chief founder of the National Republican, or Whig, party.

Between 1836 and the coming of the Civil War, Democrats and Whigs struggled for control of the presidency and of Congress. Third parties appeared occasionally. The Democratic party outlasted the Whig party, which was replaced in 1856 by the new Republican party.

► Look at the tables on page C-36, showing the presidential elections, 1836 and 1840. Compare them with the tables for 1828 and 1832 on pages C-24 and C-34. Which states were most consistently for Democratic candidates?

● Was either party nationally opposed to slavery? Which party might be antislavery in certain sections? Which sections?

● In which election had the Jacksonian coalition clearly broken down?

● What might happen to the United States if one party or more became sectional, not national, in its appeal and its political base?

★ You may find it useful to trace several outline maps of the United States, and shade in different colors the states won by the candidates in 1828, 1832, 1836, and 1840.

★ Investigate the most recent presidential election. Which states went for which party? What parts of the country are each party's main power base? Can you identify any coalitions of interests or geographic sections?

After Jackson's retirement to his Tennessee plantation in 1837, leaders of his party were elected to the presidency in four of the six elections before the Civil War. The four Jacksonian presidents—Martin Van Buren (1837–41), James K. Polk (1845–49), Franklin Pierce (1853–57), and James Buchanan (1857–61)—all had held federal offices during Jackson's presidency. Van Buren and Polk were picked for the White House by Jackson himself.

Of these four, Polk was the most vigorous executive. The four came from every region of the country except the lower South. All sought to carry out policies initiated by Jackson; all faced the difficult task of satisfying the various powerful interests within their party's coalition.

● The period between 1800 and 1824 sometimes has been called the time of the "Virginia dynasty." How might a comparison of the Virginia dynasty with the Jacksonian dynasty suggest a strong change in American political circumstances? (Consider, for instance, what this change signified as to the relative political power of Virginia.)

The Whig Interludes

The Whig party owed its very existence to Henry Clay. It gave him its presidential nomination in 1832, when it still was known as the National Republican party. It gave him the nomination again in 1844, and again he went down to defeat, this time at the hand of James K. Polk of Tennessee. Clay had the clearest program for national action of any candidate since

President 1837-1841

Martin Van Buren

President 1845-1849

James K. Polk

President 1853-1857

Franklin S. Pierce

President 1857-1861

James Buchanan

Thomas Jefferson. This program, "The American System," seemed to offer something for almost everyone. But also it offered something to antagonize almost every interest.

● Is it always wise for a presidential candidate to tell the public precise details of his plans? Might such candor sometimes make a candidate "unelectable"?

The Whigs did manage to elect two presidents between the years 1828 and 1850. They achieved this by learning well the political lesson of 1828. Popular democracy demanded new campaign tactics. If the Jacksonians could use posters, parades, and slander to elect a candidate, so could the Whigs.

In 1840 President Van Buren stood for reelection. The Whigs nominated William Henry Harrison of Ohio. Van Buren had done much in the campaigns that elected Jackson. Now he found his tactics turned against him. Van Buren had a serious disadvantage in this election. As president he inherited the disastrous economic depression resulting in a large measure from Jackson's banking and monetary policies. By 1840 large numbers of people were ruined or unemployed. It would have been difficult for any president to be reelected under these circumstances.

Van Buren's Whig opponent was a general who had distinguished himself in wars against the Indians. Like Adams, Van Buren was called an aristocrat by his opponents. Whigs declared that Van Buren was extravagant, drinking champagne and dining off golden plates, while Harrison was a simple frontiersman, happy in a log cabin with a jug of cider at his elbow. There was little truth in any of this—Harrison came from a background of affluence and owned much land—but, as Van Buren found out, the facts could be forgotten and twisted in the heat of a campaign. "Little Van, the used-up man" went down to defeat.

● "Old Tippecanoe," as Harrison was called, earned his reputation and his nickname in the frontier wars. Why would renown as an Indian-fighter be helpful to a candidate of the 1840's?

● Harrison, like Jackson, was a military hero not closely associated with any political program. Why have such men made attractive political candidates often in American history?

The country had no opportunity to discover what sort of president William Henry Harrison might have made. He was old at the time of his election. The strain of the campaign had worn him out, and he died, one month to the day, after his inauguration. John Tyler, of Virginia, his vice-president, succeeded him in office. Soon Tyler quarreled with Clay and other Whig leaders, and was repudiated by many in his own party.

In 1848 a second Whig presidential victory was followed by a similar series of events. Again the Whigs nominated a military man, "Rough and Ready" Zachary Taylor. Again the new president died in office, to be succeeded by his vice-president, Millard Fillmore of New York—a pleasant but untalented man.

● Harrison was the first president to die in office. Whig leaders believed that Tyler, whom they called "His Accidency" after he began to quarrel with them, was honor-bound to carry out the program of Harrison and the Whig leadership. Tyler believed that he had the right and the duty to make his own decisions. Who was right?

● This chapter has been concerned with the challenge of democracy. How would you judge the record of the generation of 1825–50 in domestic politics? Note that many other challenges and developments are still to be examined: economic and social changes, and manifest destiny, in particular.

Economic Development

1.   *Population*

1820   [bar] 9.6 million

1850   [bar] 23.1 million

2.   *Urban Population* (people living in towns of 2,500 or more)

1820   [bar] 693,000 (7.2%)

1850   [bar] 3.5 million (15.3%)

3.   *Transportation*

By 1850 there were over 3,000 miles of canals and 9,000 miles of railroad. In 1825 there were no railroads and only the Erie Canal was in operation.

4.   *Coal*

1830   100,000 tons

1850   6 million tons

5.   *Raw Cotton*

1820   335,000 bales

1850   2,136,000 bales

6.   *Pig Iron*

1828   146,000 long tons

1850   631,000 long tons

7.   *Wheat* (no figures available before 1839)

1839   85 million bushels

1849   100.5 million bushels

8.   *Imports and Exports*

	Imports	Exports
1825	96 million dollars	100 million dollars
1850	179 million dollars	152 million dollars

9.   *Labor Force* (the figures do not include slaves)

	Farm	Nonfarm
1830	2,069,000	812,000
1850	4,902,000	2,795,000

(Source: U.S. Bureau of the Census, *Historical Abstract of the United States: Colonial Times to 1957,* Washington, D.C., U.S. Government Printing Office, 1960.)

2
New Economic Directions

How the Lives of Americans Changed

During the second quarter of the nineteenth century, the United States was a developing country. It was in the stage of development that economists call the *take-off* stage. That means the early phase of capital accumulation and industrial development. By 1849 there were more than 123,000 manufacturing businesses in the country. This figure included hand-workshops as well as factories. But factories grew very rapidly, and by 1860 the United States was second only to Great Britain in industrial production.

► Look at the statistics showing economic development on page C-40. Did the production of coal and pig iron grow faster than population?

► How did the growth of *urban* population compare with the growth of population as a whole?

► Did the U.S.A. import more than it exported during this period?

► Did the proportion of free farm workers compared to free nonfarm workers change during the period? Explain.

● Was the United States predominantly an agricultural or an industrial country in 1850?

The Challenge to Rural America

Thomas Jefferson, writing not long after the Revolution, had declared in his *Notes on the State of Virginia* that "those who labor in the earth are the chosen people of God, if ever he had a chosen people, whose breasts he has made his peculiar deposit for substantial and genuine virtue." Yet the rural America that Jefferson praised began to retreat before a new economic order. By the time of his death, in 1826, Jefferson had ceased to hope that Americans might remain an agricultural people primarily. During the period 1825–50, the large majority of Americans still cultivated the soil, but they had given ground before the advance of commerce and industry.

There is a word to describe the view of the good society that Jefferson held, and that word is *agrarian* meaning agricultural, or something connected with farmers. Agrarians like Jefferson believe that a country's prosperity, and its moral character, and even its freedom, depend upon healthy rural life. At best, the agrarians argue, cities are necessary evils. Agrarians look upon urban life with suspicion: the city breeds crime, vice, and idleness, they say. Also the agrarians of Jefferson's Virginia advanced economic arguments in favor of an agricultural economy and a society based upon the land, as opposed to the city-dominated societies of eighteenth- and nineteenth-century Europe.

Number of Urban Places 1820-50

	1820	1850
Places of 500,000-1,000,000	—	1
Places of 250,000-500,000	—	—
Places of 100,000-250,000	1	5
Places of 50,000-100,000	2	4
Places of 25,000-50,000	2	16
Places of 10,000-25,000	8	36
Places of 5,000-10,000	22	85
Places of 2,500-5,000	26	89
Total	61	236

(Source: *Historical Statistics of the United States, op. cit.,* p. 14.)

● To what extent do Americans still believe that rural people are more honest and virtuous than are city dwellers?

● How might popular distrust of urban life affect the way Americans approach the problems of the cities? Would this distrust help or hinder the search for solutions to urban difficulties?

Until well after the Civil War, the United States remained predominantly rural. As late as 1870, only 20 per cent of the population lived in urban areas. Yet during the period between 1825 and 1850, big towns grew. In 1800 only three out of every 1,000 Americans lived in cities of more than 10,000 population. In 1860, 150 out of every 1,000 people lived in cities that big or bigger.

► Look at the tables showing number of urban places and population by sections on pages C-42 and C-43. By how many did the number of urban places rise between 1820 and 1850?

► Which section had the largest population in 1820? Which in 1850? What was the difference between their populations in 1820 and 1850?

► Assuming that the *North* includes New England, Middle Atlantic, and East and West North Central, and the *South* the South Atlantic, and East and West South Central, what were the total populations of North and South in 1820 and in 1850?

● Do you think towns and cities grew faster in the North or the South? Why?

Industrial Towns

During the second quarter of the nineteenth century, industrial towns began to grow along the rivers of the New England states, especially Massachusetts. Some of the rural regions of Vermont and New Hampshire lost population, as their residents were attracted by the economic opportunities of such factory towns as Lowell, Massachusetts.

► Why were early industrial towns usually situated on rivers, often near a waterfall?

The town of Lowell was incorporated in 1826. In its early years, milling cotton was Lowell's chief industry. In 1850 cotton mills still were important in Lowell's economy. Many of these factories were large. One employed more than 1,200 workers. Yet cotton did not dominate Lowell's economy as it had in the beginning: the economy of Lowell had been *diversified.* By 1846 Lowell made dozens of different industrial products—mus-

Population by Sections 1820-50

	1820	1850
New England (six states)	1,660,071	2,728,116
Middle Atlantic (New York, New Jersey, Pennsylvania)	2,699,845	5,898,735
East North Central (Ohio, Indiana, Illinois, Michigan, Wisconsin)	792,719	4,523,260
West North Central (Minnesota, Iowa, Missouri)	66,586	880,335
South Atlantic (seven states, Delaware to Florida, and D.C.)	3,061,063	4,679,090
East South Central (Kentucky, Tennessee, Alabama, Mississippi)	1,190,489	3,363,271
West South Central (Arkansas, Louisiana, Oklahoma, Texas)	167,680	940,251
Mountain (New Mexico, Utah)	——	72,927
Pacific (Washington, Oregon, California)	——	105,891

(Source: *Historical Statistics, op. cit.,* p. 13.)

lins, wrapping papers, window shades, harness leathers, trunks, epsom salts, mustard, chocolate, rice flour, steel pens, brass wire, school slates, locks, house bells, ice-cream freezers, washing machines, bullet molds, water filters, steam boilers, seed planters, threshing machines, bath heaters, tobacco presses, reaping machines, cotton looms, card-making machines, pumps, and others.

● Is it an advantage for a community to have a diversified economy? Is a diversified economy more or less likely to experience strain during a period of economic change?

Lowell was only one of many manufacturing centers that appeared in the New England states, the Middle Atlantic states, and even some of the newer states of the

A view of the textile center at Lawrence, Massachusetts

West, during the period 1825–50. As Alexander Hamilton had said, the Americans were an inventive people.

Discovering New Processes and Machines

Many industrial processes that we now take for granted, and machines that make a developed economy possible, originated in the United States during the second quarter of the nineteenth century. As late as 1820, the United States Patent Office was issuing annually only some 200 patents for new inventions. But by the time of the Civil War, several thousand patents were being issued every year. Invention usually requires hard work and imagination, and perhaps luck. Many of the inventors active before the Civil War were men of little formal training. They came upon their inventions, sometimes, by trial and error. Few discoveries are made overnight.

Charles Goodyear (1800–60) was the son of a man who enjoyed tinkering with things. About 1830 rubber began to be imported into the United States. This flexible, waterproof substance seemed to offer manufacturers a chance at a fortune. And for a few years, the country experienced a rubber boom. But soon it was found that natural rubber presented difficulties: in hot weather the material might melt into a sticky mess. Many men looked for ways to cure rubber of this trouble — but without success.

Goodyear took up the problem in 1834. He began by experimenting with combinations of rubber and other substances, unsuccessfully. Obsessed by such matters, he neglected to earn a living for his family. From time to time, he was committed to a debtors' prison, but continued his experiments even in jail. At the end of five years, Goodyear seemed no closer to solving this puzzling problem. But one day, while experimenting with a mixture of rubber and sulfur, he accidentally dropped some of the mixture on a hot stove. Goodyear thus discovered *vulcanization* — the process by which rubber, treated with sulfur, and heated, forms a product unaffected by temperature or humidity.

Several more years were required for experimenting to determine the proper proportions and temperature. Goodyear patented his process in 1844. Unhappily for himself and his family, his years of research left him so deeply in debt that he was forced to sell licenses for the process very cheaply. When he died, he was more than $200,000 in debt.

Some inventors made a great deal of money. Cyrus Hall McCormick (1809–84) was the most eminent of these. McCormick's father spent many years in trying to devise a machine that would harvest mechanically such grains as wheats, oats, and rye. A mechanical reaper was much needed. The cereal grains require two periods of intensive labor every year — planting and harvest. During the rest of the year, a farmer may spend most of his time at other chores. The harvest season is especially critical, for the fields of grain ripen all at once. They must be harvested swiftly, before bad weather can

American Inventions and Improvements in Technology, 1825-50

1827-1831	Joseph Henry produces insulated wire and basis for electric telegraph
1828	First indoor plumbing
1831	Introduction of the daguerreotype (earliest photograph)
1830	Peter Cooper builds the first American locomotive
1833	John Lane's steel-blade plow
1833-40	Development of blast furnace for smelting iron
1834	McCormick's reaper
1835	Mass production of straight pins; Colt's revolver
1836	Hiram and John Pitt's thresher
1839	Goodyear vulcanizes rubber
1837-40	John Deere's improved steel plow
1840	Norbert Rillieux, a black, invented a vacuum evaporator for sugar refining
1842	Invention of the grain elevator by Joseph Dart
1844	Morse's telegraph: Baltimore-Washington
1846	Roebling's suspension bridges at Pittsburgh and Niagara
1846-54	Sewing machine (Howe, Wilson, and Singer)
1850	Factory production of left and right shoes
	Mass production of clocks by Chauncey Jerome

ruin them. Thus harvest time was then a period of severe labor shortage. The limiting factor on grain production was the labor force available at harvest season.

Learning from his father's failures, McCormick set to work on the problem. In 1834 he patented an efficient reaping machine. From that time to this, the reaping process has remained basically the same—except that new sources of power for machines have been found, and refinements have been made in ways to gather the grain. Deciding to capture a large market for his invention, McCormick built a factory in Chicago in 1847. By 1848, when his original patent expired, McCormick was well on his way to becoming the wealthiest industrialist of his generation.

● Why do you suppose that McCormick chose Chicago as the site for his factory?

(Top left) Goodyear vulcanizes rubber; (Top right) Singer's sewing machine; (Below) Cyrus McCormick's first reaper

● In 1848, when McCormick's patent was still in effect, there were only two manufacturers of mechanical reapers. (Their machines were constructed on different principles, and McCormick's was superior.) By 1850 there were thirty manufacturers of reapers, and by 1860 McCormick had more than a hundred competitors. Do you think that the patent rights helped or hindered the introduction of mechanical harvesting?

● Some historians say that McCormick's reaper made it possible for the North to win the Civil War—although McCormick himself sympathized with the South. How do they come to this conclusion?

Fairly often, useful inventions resulted from the contributions of several inventors. The sewing machine is one example. Elias Howe (1819–67) patented a working model of such a machine in 1846. This particular machine did not sell well, but once its basic principle became known, many competing machines appeared. Isaac Singer (1811–75) vastly improved upon Howe's machine, and obtained a patent in 1851. In the end, both inventors grew rich.

▶ How did the sewing machine affect the lives of ordinary Americans?

Technology, rather than pure science, prospered in America during this period—a fact remarked by Alexis de Tocqueville, the shrewdest European observer of American society at that time. Often Americans would take notice of some scientific principle discovered in Europe much earlier, but never practically applied in Europe. Then America's "Yankee tinkers" would discover ways to put such principles or devices to practical use.

One instance of this genius for practical application was the *anaesthetic*, or pain-killer, called ether $(C_2H_5)_2O$, a liquid readily turned into a gas. Ether was discovered in England late in the eighteenth century. But until the American talent for practical uses went to work, ether was a scientific curiosity or mere toy, not employed in regular medical practice. Independently, two American medical men found that ether could be used to relieve patients from pain during surgical operations. One of them was a Georgia physician, Crawford Long, who by 1846 had performed six such operations under ether anaesthesia. The other was a Massachusetts dentist, William T. G. Morton, who applied ether to both dentistry and surgery, and patented his invention in 1846. The employment of ether in scientific medicine then spread swiftly to all civilized lands, and the age of painless surgery began.

★ An English surgeon and scientist, Joseph Lister, made a discovery not long after the use of ether came into practice. His discovery made surgery far safer. What was it?

Sometimes inventions in apparently unrelated fields made one another more useful. Samuel F. B. Morse (1791–1872) became both a scientist and an inventor. He was well educated, a graduate of Yale College. Throughout his life, art was his first love, and he became well known on both sides of the Atlantic as a painter of portraits and historical scenes. About 1829 Morse became interested in electricity. In 1832 he took up a lively problem. It had been demonstrated that an electric current could be sent along a wire, and Morse thought that a way might be found to use this current for sending messages over long distances.

Before Morse's concept could take on reality, four problems had to be solved. A way for sending messages had to be devised, and also a way for receiving them at the other end. Further, because electrical signals weakened over long distances, a signal *booster* had to be contrived. Finally, a "language" had to be invented, because no one had yet discovered a means for transmitting the human voice. By 1836 Morse had constructed a working model of his invention, and had invented a language—now called the Morse Code —for sending messages. He patented these in 1837.

Morse conducted some of his early experiments in a room with ten miles of wire circling its walls. Before the usefulness of his scheme could be established, demonstration on a larger scale was necessary. For six years, Morse and his friends asked Congress for funds. Their labors were rewarded when $30,000 was appropriated for this research in 1843. Morse used the money to construct a telegraph line from Washington to Baltimore. In 1844 he transmitted the first telegraph message, "What hath God wrought."

Happily for Morse and his telegraph, technological change already was creating a demand for speedier communication of news. The first American newspapers had appeared in the colonial era. In those days, and well into the nineteenth century, printing was a slow process requiring much manual labor. Papers were therefore small and expensive. The introduction of the steam-powered press was an improvement, but as late as 1830 the best presses could produce only 2,000 printings an hour.

Among the major manufacturers of printing presses was the Hoe Company. Richard Hoe (1812–66) was a successful industrialist as well as a clever inventor. By the middle 1840's, Hoe had invented a printing press that could print as many as ten copies of a page of type at the same time. In 1847 the *Philadelphia Ledger* began printing its newspapers on the new Hoe presses, at the rate of 8,000 copies an hour. Some newspapers commenced to print more than one edition a day. Newspapers ceased to be a luxury at six cents a copy. Instead, the penny press arrived, and newspapers became part of the daily life of many thousands of Americans.

How could news be obtained swiftly by the newspapers? Hitherto, news had been transmitted only by ship, by horseman, by postman on foot, or at best by railroad train. Now Morse's telegraph became the means for supplying the newspapers with speedy reports from many parts of the world—as well as the chief instrument for sending private messages in haste.

● Explain in your own words how developments in printing and telegraphy stimulated each other.

● What other groups in American society could be expected to benefit from rapid communications, and how?

★ In 1857 Samuel F. B. Morse proposed to an American industrialist, Cyrus W. Field, a project that much enlarged the field of telegraphy. See if you can discover what that project was.

★ Two successful inventors about the middle of the twentieth century were Edwin H. Land (Polaroid cameras) and Chester F. Carlson (the Xerox reproduction process). Investigate these men and their inventions. What do their careers have in common with the careers of the nineteenth-century inventors we have just studied? What differences do you notice?

★ Look at the list on page C-45 of some American inventions and technological improvements, from 1825–50. Discuss the importance of those not mentioned in the text above.

● How did the developments described above affect the lives of ordinary men and women? For example, how would McCormick's reaper affect the standard of living of Americans and of Europeans? How would anaesthesia affect health and expectation of life?

New Transportation, by Water and Land

Technological progress increased the amount and variety of goods available to Americans. Also, technology brought a revolution in the way goods were shipped. Without a strong improvement in America's system of transportation, economic growth would have been difficult in this vast country, with its mountains, forests, and great rivers.

From 1825 to 1840, many canals were built. The first was the Erie Canal, which opened up the Great Lakes region and made New York City the most important port and commercial center of the United States. Other states contracted "canal fever" — Ohio, Pennsylvania, Maryland, Indiana. By 1838 twelve states had contracted debts for canals amounting to more that $60 million. Canal fever, however, could be a dangerous disease: projects were adopted in haste, without much thought about their practicability. In the decade of the 1840's, four states nearly went bankrupt because of excessive debts for these projects.[1]

The steamboat, too, came of age in the 1825–50 generation. Early steam vessels were built to operate on eastern rivers. They had deep hulls, and carried most of their cargo below decks. They were able to operate with low-pressure steam engines, and frequently carried sails also. Steamboats built for western rivers were considerably different. Their hulls were flat and shallow, and the superstruc-

[1] For more about canals, see Unit 4, "*The Young Nation, 1800–25,*" in *The American Adventure: The Forming of the Republic* (Boston: Allyn and Bacon, 1973), pp. B-187–B-189.

ture — the part of the vessel above the deck — sometimes was three stories high. Low-pressure engines could not be used: the far more powerful (and dangerous) high-pressure engines were installed above the waterline, and fuel, cargo, and passengers all were carried on the main deck and the superstructure. Hundreds of such craft steamed up and down the Mississippi and Ohio river systems. Competition was ruthless, so that captains sometimes forced the last ounce of speed out of their vessels. Collisions and boiler explosions occurred frequently, costing many lives.

● Consider the differences in design between eastern and western steamboats. What do these differences suggest about the nature of the rivers they were meant to operate in? Consider river depth and swiftness of currents.

Although canals and steamboats mightily improved America's transportation system, great regions of the country could not be reached by water. Land transportation had not improved significantly since the time of the Roman Empire. Men still were limited to what could be carried or pulled by horses, oxen, and other beasts of burden. In many parts of the United States about 1825, land transportation was not as good as it had been in the Roman Empire about the time of the birth of Jesus (Christ).

Both federal and state governments were improving roads in the 1820's and 1830's. In 1824 Congress authorized a general survey of the need for new turnpikes and canals. The "National Road," or "Cumberland Road," intended to open the way to the West, received large appropriations from Congress in 1825. This highway of crushed stone was gradually extended across Ohio, Indiana, and Illinois, and it was meant to extend to Jefferson City, Missouri. Some people hoped that eventually it would run all the way to

(Left) A Mississippi River steamboat

(Right) An Eastern river steamboat

Santa Fe, New Mexico. However, when the National Road reached Vandalia, Illinois, in 1838, construction was halted. President Jackson suspended work on the National Road not merely because he disapproved of "internal improvements" at federal expense, but also because by 1838 it was clear that wagon roads could not compete with a new means of transportation. For the "Railway Age" had commenced.

First developed in England railroads promptly were built by the Americans. The new steam-driven railways were far swifter than canal barges or horse-drawn wagons. American men of business were quick to recognize the promise of railroads, and by 1830 several companies had been formed to construct railroad lines in the United States. Both the South Carolina Railroad and the Baltimore and Ohio Railroad, America's earliest lines, commenced operations in 1830. The first American locomotive engines were built

and delivered in the same year. Most of the early railroads were short lines—the longest in the United States was also the longest in the world, 136 miles. Railway development proceeded rapidly. In the first six years, more than a thousand miles of track were laid, and railroads began to run trains in eleven states.

● Look at the map, on page C-52 "Railroads, 1850." As you can see by the map, short railroad lines were scattered throughout most of the Eastern states. Can you think of a reason for this pattern of development? What other transportation system might railroads have been built to supplement?

In the 1850's, rail service was extended to the Mississippi River. Except for the bulkiest of goods, railroads became the most economical form of transportation within the United States. Traveling by

Cumberland Road or the National Turnpike

water between New York City and Detroit in the 1850's took ten days; by rail, the same trip required only four days.

Railroads were not popular with everybody. Farmers complained that the noise frightened their cattle, and that sparks from the engines set their fields afire. Some physicians feared that the human body could not endure travel at speeds so high as 30 miles an hour. Canal companies tried to keep railroads from building lines that might compete with canals. Nevertheless, the usefulness of railroads overcame public resistance, and people put up with discomfort and danger to ride the new contraptions. An English-woman travelling in America in 1835 described some of the troubles of her trip:

One great inconvenience of the American railroads is that from wood being used as fuel, there is an incessant shower of large sparks, destructive to dress and comfort, unless all windows are shut, which is impossible in warm weather. Some serious accidents from fire have happened in this way; and during my last trip on the Columbia and Philadelphia railroad, a lady in the car had a shawl burned to destruction on her shoulders; and I found that my own gown had thirteen holes in it; and my veil, with which I saved my eyes, more than could be counted.[2]

● Look at the illustrations on page C-53 comparing trains c. 1830 and 1950. What major improvements had obviously been made over the 120 years of operation? Can you see how early designers could not break away from patterns suited to a quite different form of transportation?

★ The period 1825–50 saw the development of the highest achievement

[2]Harriet Martineau, *Society in America* [1836], cited in T. H. Williams, *et al., A History of the United States,* Vol. I (2d ed.; New York: Knopf, 1969), p. 351.

RAILROADS, 1850

in sailing-ship technology, the great "clipper ships." Find out something about them—how fast they were, on what trade routes they were used, and similar details. The same period saw the beginning of technological advances that ended the "Age of Sail." What were these?

By the end of the generation of 1825–50, the railroads carried settlers and their goods right to the Mississippi River.

During the Civil War the American railroad network brought great changes in military strategy. By 1869 the first transcontinental railroad was completed.

The Growth of Corporations

Railroads could make great profits. However, no other business enterprise needed so much capital outlay. Land had to be purchased for rights of way. Rails had to be bought and laid. Bridges and tunnels had to be built. Rolling stock had to be purchased, and train crews hired, before the railway companies could begin to operate.

Fortunately, a new form of business organization had been developed. This was the *limited liability corporation*.[3] The corporation was similar in some ways to the older *joint-stock company*. However, the new corporation was based on the new principle of limited liability.

★ What is *limited liability?* How does it protect investors? Does it encourage persons with relatively small savings to invest in businesses? Explain.

★ How does a limited liability corporation differ from a *partnership* from the legal point of view?

● Why was a device needed at this time to raise large amounts of capital for investment?

● Do you think that the device of the limited liability corporation might lead to abuses? For example: excessive speculation, financial and managerial irresponsibility, deception of investors, corruption? Explain. Might the existence of big corporations make economic crises or depressions more disastrous when they occurred? Why or why not?

● Do the holders of stock in a corporation (common stockholders) exercise any control over the corporation? How? How are votes counted at a meeting of stockholders? At first glance a corporation may appear to be "democratically" controlled. In fact, however, corporations often led to the concentration of economic power in the hands of a few businessmen. How could that happen?

[3]See Unit 4, "*The Young Nation, 1800–25*" in *The American Adventure: The Forming of The Republic* (Boston: Allyn and Bacon, 1973), p. B-109.

(Left) An 1838 steam engine in the Mohawk Valley in New York
(Right) The "Super Chief", a pullman streamliner ran between Chicago and Los Angeles in 1950

● Look at Marshall's definition of a corporation on page C-55. Explain what he means by "an artificial being" with "immortality" and "individuality." What might states do, when granting charters of incorporation, to keep some control over corporations?

● It has been suggested that but for Marshall's *Dartmouth College* decision, the United States might have remained an agricultural nation, without big industrial enterprises. Do you agree? Why or why not?

In 1800 there were more than 300 corporations in the United States, only six of which were engaged in manufacturing. As the years passed, both the number and the size of corporations increased, and more of them were manufacturing concerns. By 1833 at least one textile manufacturing company had capital stock valued at a million dollars.

● By the time of the Civil War, all major railroad companies were corporations. The New York Central Railroad was incorporated in 1853. Along the route between Albany and Buffalo, ten small railroads were merged to form the new company. Its stock was valued at $34 million and there were 2,455 stockholders. Explain why a partnership would have been impractical for an enterprise of this scale.

Depression

It must not be forgotten that the United States had its worst economic depression (to date) during this period. There had been many ups-and-downs of the business cycle since the achievement of independence. The last depression had occurred in 1819–22.

In 1837, as has already been pointed out, a severe panic and crisis struck the country.[4] It followed a period of wild speculation in land and of *easy money* (easy credit) provided by many state banks that inherited the government deposits of the Bank of the United States. President Jackson and his advisers decided to apply the brakes to the economy by insisting that purchases of land be paid for in hard money. The remedy was, apparently, too sudden. Land values collapsed. Stocks went down. Prices of goods fell steeply. Many banks failed. Many foreign investors—especially British investors—lost millions and millions of dollars. Unemployment spread. The old Bank of the United States (now a Pennsylvania corporation) went bankrupt in 1839. Not until 1844 did the economy of the United States begin to recover.

★ The crisis spread to Europe. In Britain the 1840's were called "the Hungry Forties." Why? There were also many revolutionary movements in Europe at this time. Find out about the Chartists. Why was 1848 known as the "Year of Revolutions"? When did Karl Marx and Friedrich Engels publish the *Communist Manifesto*?

Agriculture and Industry

By 1850 the foundations of America's industrial power had been laid. Capital investment was increasing rapidly. A new breed of industrial and financial leaders was coming to the fore. Many were millionaires. John Jacob Astor, who made his fortune in fur-trading, was worth $20 million when he died in 1848. Cornelius Vanderbilt, the railroad king of the 1870's, had made a fortune in shipping by 1850. Andrew Carnegie, the future steel magnate, was only a telegraph operator in

---

[4]See p. C-35.

Chief Justice Marshall Defines a Corporation

In the *Dartmouth College* Case, 1819, Chief Justice Marshall gave the following definition of a corporation. In this case he was speaking of a chartered, incorporated educational institution. However, his definition could be and was applied to business corporations, too.

A corporation is an artificial being, invisible, intangible, and existing only in contemplation of the law. Being a mere creature of the law, it possesses only those properties which the charter of its creation confers upon it either expressly or as incidental to its very existence. These are such as are supposed best calculated to effect the object for which it was created. Among the more important are immortality, and, if the expression may be allowed, individuality: properties by which a perpetual succession of persons are considered as the same, and may act as a single individual. They enable a corporation to manage its own affairs, and to hold property without the perplexing intricacies, the hazardous and endless necessity, of perpetual conveyances for the purpose of transmitting it from hand to hand.

1850, but was destined to rise rapidly in power and wealth. Cyrus McCormick, in the same year, had just established his great business in farm machinery. These men were typical of the entrepreneurs whose personalities dominated the industrialization of the United States.

Yet the country, in 1850, was still an agricultural country. Farm families made up 80 per cent of the population. Agricultural products were the country's vital exports. Of industrial developments between 1825 and 1850, by far the most important were those that improved farm production—especially reapers and steel plows. Mechanical threshers, seed drills, and cultivators came in the 1840's. Grain elevators also appeared during this decade. The railroad's great service was to bring wheat and other agricultural products to Eastern markets. An efficient, prosperous agriculture was the essential base for the industrial power of the later nineteenth century.

The Mississippi River

3

The Mississippi Frontier, 1825-35

Consolidation

The last few years of the generation of 1825–50 saw an astounding burst of expansion. For a time, however, it seemed as if Americans were content to settle and secure the Louisiana Territory and the newly acquired lands of Florida. Perhaps the settled frontier of the United States would stabilize along the Mississippi. Or would pioneers push on—"'cross the wide Missouri"?

A Pause at the Mississippi

Until 1820, the westward movement was directed mainly to settling the region between the Appalachian Mountains and the Mississippi. By 1819, most of that land had been organized into states. One state already existed west of the Mississippi. This trans-Mississippi state, Louisiana, together with seven others west of the Appalachians, had a total population of 2,200,000 people. East of the Mississippi, only the territories that are now the states of Michigan and Wisconsin remained largely unsettled.

One other territory west of the Mississippi was also settled by 1820. This was the territory that became the state of Missouri in 1821.

Meanwhile, the United States acquired Florida in 1819. Andrew Jackson, as the new governor of Florida, received the Spanish surrender of that province in the summer of 1821. When Mexico obtained independence from Spain that same year, Spanish power vanished from Texas, New Mexico, and (soon thereafter) California. Would the new Mexican Republic be strong enough to oppose expansion into the Southwest by citizens of the United States?

Beyond the Mississippi were many great Indian peoples. On the Great Plains (then called the "Great American Desert") there roved the Crow, the Blackfeet, the Comanche, and nearly 30 more major tribes. On the Plains were also the territories loosely dominated by the Dakota (or Sioux) confederation. To the southwest lived the Navajo, Apache, and Pueblo peoples. Finally, near the Pacific coast were many more Indian peoples, including the Yakima, Nootka, Kwakiutl, and Yurok. Most of these peoples were poorly armed though courageous. They lacked any sort of unity, and in many cases fought wars with one another.

★ By 1825 the Plains Indians were far more prosperous and powerful than they had been a century earlier. What new technology had they acquired? How had they acquired it?

(Top) Buffalo herds on the Plains
(Below) An Omaha Indian reports
to Young Elk, his chief

As late as 1835, the American government had no clear intention of settling all the lands beyond the Mississippi. Americans, except for some traders and trappers who wandered the plains or traveled as far as New Mexico and Oregon, thought of the Great Plains as a real desert, virtually worthless. There still was plenty of land for homesteading east of the great river. After Missouri, with a population of 66,000 settlers, had become a state, there was no general push of settlers westward for some years.

The Expulsion of Eastern Indians

If the United States had any use for the Great American Desert, it was as a region to which the Eastern Indians could be sent—thus clearing the way for white settlement of lands east of the Mississippi.

When Andrew Jackson, that old Indian-fighter, came to the White House, he agreed with John C. Calhoun, his vice-president, that the eastern Indians ought to be removed beyond the Mississippi River.

President John Quincy Adams had tried in vain to protect the Indians' rights under treaties with the United States. But already the Indians were under heavy pressure to depart. Many white citizens, especially in Georgia, Alabama, Mississippi, Florida, and Tennessee, were thrusting the Indians off lands that had been guaranteed to them by treaty. This process went on for nearly half a century—more rapidly in the North than in the South. The last Northern military campaign against Eastern Indians occurred in 1832, when the Sac and Fox Indians of northern Illinois were crushed in the *Black Hawk War*. Perhaps a hundred thousand Indians were forced to retreat across the Mississippi.

In the Southern states dwelt the so-called "Five Civilized Tribes"—Creeks, Cherokees, Choctaws, Chickasaws, and Seminoles. Missionaries had converted many of them to Christianity, and Congress had appropriated small sums of money for a "Civilization Fund." These Indian peoples lived in well-established communities, raised crops and livestock, and engaged in trade. Many of their leading men—who often bore Scottish or Scotch-Irish surnames—owned black slaves. The Cherokees had developed their own written language, and published their own newspaper. In many respects, these "civilized" Indians adopted the white men's political institutions. Indeed, many of them had a strong strain of European blood; John Ross, the greatest Cherokee chief from 1828 to 1866, was one-eighth Cherokee and seven-eighths white.

All this did not save them. Most of

The Trail of Tears—Indians in the East were forced to move West with much suffering and with only what they could carry

their white neighbors looked upon the Civilized Tribes as savages who were still potentially dangerous. Besides, the new railroads and highways would have to pass through the lands of these tribes. State governments were more and more opposed to independent Indian sovereignties within their state boundaries. President Jackson believed that white man and red man could not live satisfactorily side by side. Either the Indians must be wiped out, or else they must migrate to regions where few or no white settlements existed. He was willing to permit the state governments to deal with these tribes as they wished.

Shortly after Jackson's election, the Georgia legislature passed an act declaring that thereafter all Indians in the "Cherokee Territory" would be subject to the laws of Georgia. This meant that the Indian tribes were not independent nations, and that the statutes of the Cherokee government were null and void. The Creeks already had been compelled to migrate westward, with much suffering, and the Seminoles of Florida were expected to shift across the Mississippi, too. There remained the Cherokees and the Choctaw and Chickasaw tribes. Georgia and other state governments declared that they must depart promptly for the West.

The Indians had one possible protector—Chief Justice John Marshall, President Jackson's political enemy. When an unruly crowd of white Georgians poured into Cherokee Territory, in search of gold (discovered there in 1829), the alarmed Cherokees appealed to the Supreme Court of the United States. In January 1831, Chief Justice Marshall handed down the Court's decision. The Cherokee nation was a political state, Marshall said, and yet not a "foreign state" to be dealt with through diplomacy by the federal government. Therefore, the Supreme Court could not act on an appeal that came from an Indian people who claimed to be a foreign state.

However, in 1832, the chief justice and his colleagues supported the Cherokees' argument that they were not bound by the laws of Georgia. In this case (*Worcester* v. *State of Georgia*), Georgia's officers had arrested a white Presbyterian missionary to the Cherokees. Marshall ruled that this arrest had been illegal, for the laws of Georgia did not govern the Cherokee nation, and "the citizens of Georgia have no right to enter but with the assent of the Cherokees themselves or in conformity with treaties and with acts of Congress."

Even the authority of Marshall, however, could not save the Cherokees and the other Civilized Tribes. The Georgia government ignored the Supreme Court's decision, and took no notice of the Court's attempt to save from execution a protesting Cherokee, Corn Tassel. Worcester, the Presbyterian missionary, was confined for a year in a Georgia jail, Supreme Court or no Supreme Court.

Then, as today, the Supreme Court had no troops to enforce its decisions. The president and lesser federal officials are expected to comply with the Court's rulings. Even though some of Marshall's decisions had been thoroughly unpopular with the followers of Jefferson and other Virginian presidents, they had been obeyed, out of respect for the rule of law. But President Jackson, sympathizing with the Georgians, scarcely would speak to Chief Justice Marshall. According to one report, "Old Hickory" Jackson commented sourly, "John Marshall has made his decision; now let him enforce it." Without the president's assistance, the Supreme Court was powerless. In effect, the government of Georgia had nullified treaties made by the federal government. Jackson refused to deal with nullification in Georgia as he had dealt with it in South Carolina. The Cherokee cause was lost.

In sorrow and anger, the Civilized Tribes began their long march, escorted and prodded by troops, to the empty lands along the Arkansas River, across the Mississippi. Some of the Cherokees held out until Martin Van Buren became president; then they, too, moved westward, after the government had paid them $5 million for their old homeland. Many Indians were robbed or assaulted by white adventurers who rushed in to seize their houses and farms, or to claim their livestock. The last great expulsion occurred in 1838.

In New England and other places many people pitied the Civilized Tribes. Some counties of East Tennessee protested against the roughness of the Cherokees' eviction. The United States general who was first put in charge of this "removal" was relieved of command because of his alleged sympathy with the Indians. A Tennessee general of militia declared "that he would never dishonor the Tennessee arms by aiding to carry into execution at the point of a bayonet a treaty made by a lean minority against the will and authority of the Cherokee Nation." James Mooney, an historian who studied the Cherokees in the 1880's, wrote that: "The history of the Cherokee removal of 1838, as gleaned by the author from the lips of actors in the tragedy, may well exceed the grief and pathos of any other passage in American history."

Some thousand Cherokees hid themselves in the mountains of North Carolina and Tennessee, where their descendants remain on a reservation to this day. In Florida, the Seminoles rebelled against "removal." They fought against federal troops and Florida militia from 1835 to 1842, under their heroic chief Osceola. Even when most of the nation had been removed or destroyed, a few hundred Seminoles retreated into Florida's Everglades, so that some Seminoles live in those swamps still. Except for these remnants, the Civilized Tribes were exiled to what is now Oklahoma.

Even after being resettled west of the Mississippi, the Civilized Tribes suffered grimly. The Plains Indians, resenting these newcomers, attacked them. An army column had to defend the Eastern Indians against the Kiowa, Comanche, Cheyenne, and Wichita tribes.

Although the Jackson and Van Buren administrations had intended to remove all Indians westward, the national government never completed this policy, so that small Indian reservations remain now in many Eastern states—even as far east as Cape Cod and Long Island. After 1842 the "Indian problem" survived only in the Great Plains and the Far West.

- ● Do you think that President Jackson was right in believing that two races could not live in peace side by side? Are Indian tribes still regarded in American law as "nations"?

- ★ Have any other Supreme Court decisions been ignored by a president of the United States? Marshall's decision in the *Worcester* v. *Georgia* case was unpopular with the majority of American citizens. What recent decisions of the Supreme Court have been unpopular with many citizens? Can Congress restrict the jurisdiction of the Supreme Court? (See Article III, Section 2, of the U.S. Constitution.)

- ★ Can you recall any previous treaties with Indians that were broken by white men?

The Westward Movement Resumes

As late as President Tyler's administration, the government at Washington had no intention of expanding white settlement into the Great Plains. Yet the westward movement started again. A series of Indian wars lasted from 1851 until the 1890's. According to historian

A caravan of Conestoga wagons headed for California crossing
through Nebraska in the 1840's

S. L. A. Marshall the blame lies with both sides, white and Indian:

The wars were not the poison fruit of bureaucratic negligence, nor were they strictly the evil consequence of white exploiters cheating the Plains Indian of his lawful property, though all too frequently they were given that appearance with Government giving its backing to the exploiters.

Rather, violence beset the western frontier and lasted and lasted because the fundamental interests of the two sides were so wholly irreconcilable as to leave little or no room for compromise. Due to the absence of any middle ground, there occurred intolerable grievances of white man and red. When these basic conditions are present, war or revolution becomes inevitable.[1]

---

[1]S. L. A. Marshall, *Crimsoned Prairie: The Wars Between the United States and the Plains Indians During the Winning of the West* (New York: Charles Scribner's Sons, 1972), p. 10.

Even though the national government had no intention of settling the Plains, American citizens began to surge across the "Great American Desert" in the 1840's. One reason for this was the promise of wealth beyond the Great Plains—in California and Oregon, especially. Another reason was that the question of territorial expansion became entangled with the burning dispute over slavery.

● What do you suppose were the "fundamental interests" mentioned by S. L. A. Marshall, of Indians and whites that were "irreconcilable"? The Plains Indians lived by hunting vast herds of bison: how would that means of livelihood be affected by the coming of white settlers? Why could not white men fit easily into this pattern of existence? Can you suggest any compromises that might have satisfied Indians and white men tolerably well?

Santa Fe, New Mexico, 1866

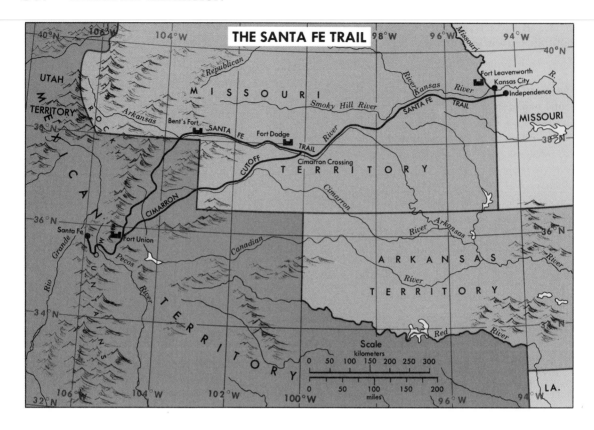

The Lure of New Mexico

As early as the 1820's, two points in the Far West acted like magnets to attract American adventurers: the Spanish town of Santa Fe, in New Mexico, and the Oregon Country, where British and American settlers and trappers lived side by side. To reach those distant regions, trails must be maintained. To protect traders against Indian bands, the American government began to establish military posts along the trails.

Spaniards had been at Santa Fe, and elsewhere in the Southwest, as long as Englishmen had been in Tidewater Virginia. But Spain's settlements in New Mexico had grown only slowly. It was some 1,500 miles from Santa Fe to Vera Cruz, Mexico's chief port. The white and Indian inhabitants of New Mexico could have traded more profitably with the

United States than with Mexico, had not the Spanish government forbidden such trade. After the Mexican Revolution, however, American traders began to find their way from Missouri to Santa Fe, joining in an annual armed caravan to barter with the New Mexicans. They sold American manufactured goods in Santa Fe, and brought back furs, mules, gold, and silver.

In 1825, Congress appropriated funds to maintain the Santa Fe Trail — including money to pay to Indian tribes, so that they would not molest caravans on the trail. Despite heavy import duties that the Mexican government tried to collect, this traffic prospered until 1843, when the president of Mexico, Santa Anna, forbade it again. Meanwhile, little forts had been built along the trail; Americans had begun to understand that the broad lands between the Missouri River and New Mexico were not worthless desert, after all; and some of

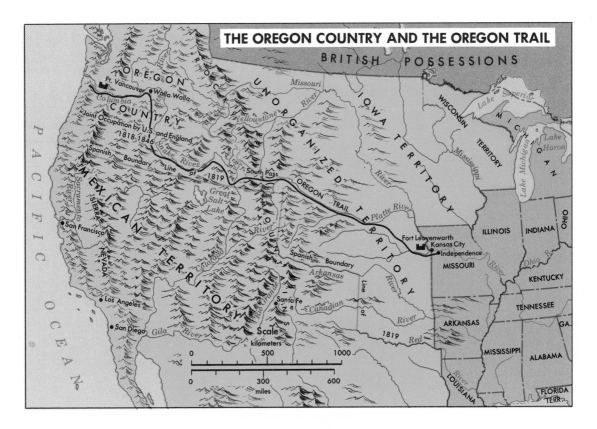

THE OREGON COUNTRY AND THE OREGON TRAIL

them had learned that Mexico probably could not hold Santa Fe, should the Americans decide to take the place.

● Why was it easier for traders to reach Santa Fe than to get to Oregon by land? Consult the map below.

The Lure of Oregon

During this same period, American traders and trappers began to move into the Oregon Country, traveling generally along the line of march that had been followed by the expedition of Lewis and Clark during Jefferson's administration. Some Americans reached Oregon by the sea route, all the way south through the Atlantic to Cape Horn, and then north along the shores of the South and North Pacific to Oregon. This was a dangerous and time-consuming voyage. A safe overland route would be preferable.

In 1818, the British and American governments agreed that the Oregon Country might be occupied by the citizens of both nations. The American Fur Company and the Rocky Mountain Fur Company, both American-owned firms but strenuously competing, sent their people into Oregon in quest of beaver and other pelts. The so-called "Mountain Men," trappers and hunters, opened up these wild territories for the fur companies. Missionaries, both Protestant and Catholic, soon followed the traders and trappers; many of the Methodist and Presbyterian missionaries to the Indians of the Northwest established farms for themselves. By the early 1840's, thousands of Americans

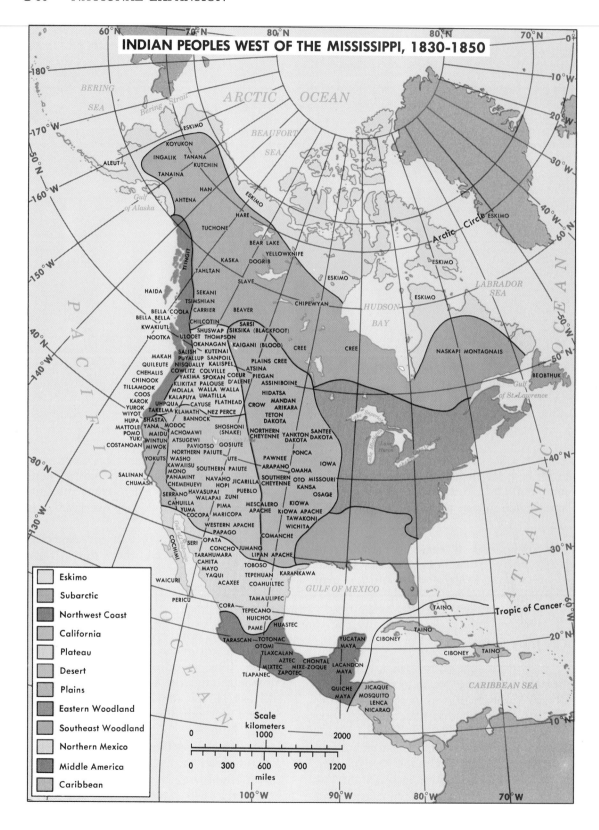

INDIAN PEOPLES WEST OF THE MISSISSIPPI, 1830-1850

Scale
kilometers

0   1000   2000

0   300   600   900   1200
miles

Legend:
- Eskimo
- Subarctic
- Northwest Coast
- California
- Plateau
- Desert
- Plains
- Eastern Woodland
- Southeast Woodland
- Northern Mexico
- Middle America
- Caribbean

had settled in Oregon, though it was not clearly American territory. The Oregon Trail was carefully surveyed in 1842.

The Oregon Trail ran across the Great Plains from the Missouri River to South Pass (now in Wyoming), and then through the Rocky Mountains to the Columbia River, in the Oregon Country. It was three times as long as the Santa Fe Trail. This Oregon Trail passed through the hunting grounds of the Sioux, Arapaho, Bannock, Shoshone, and other Indian peoples.

★ The greatest merchant of this period was John Jacob Astor, who emigrated from Germany to New York, and founded the American Fur Company in 1808. Astoria, at the mouth of the Columbia River, was one of his many trading posts. Some of his company's buildings still stand on Mackinac Island, Michigan, in the straits between Lake Michigan and Lake Huron. Where do you suppose that Astor and the other great fur traders sold their furs? Why did Astor invest his profits in New York City, rather than in the Far West?

● How would the establishment of the Oregon Trail begin to affect the lives of the Blackfoot, Sioux, and other Indian peoples along that route?

More Westward Lures

New Mexico and Oregon were calling Americans to manifest destiny. Two other areas also attracted American adventurers and pioneers. These were California and Texas. Both these areas, like New Mexico, were possessions of the young Republic of Mexico. More and more Americans saw the seizure of the great lands of the west as essential to the future of the United States. The great imperialistic drive called manifest destiny had begun.

A camp of Piegan Indians, a division of the Blackfeet, near Fort McKenzie in Wyoming

The Chronology of Manifest Destiny

1821-23	Moses and Stephen Austin lead settlers into Texas
1822-24	Expeditions to the Oregon Country
1823	The Monroe Doctrine
1832-37	Black Hawk's War and the forced removal of Indians from upper Mississippi Valley
1832-38	The Five "Civilized Tribes" forcibly moved west of the Mississippi
1835-36	War between Texans and Mexico: the Alamo; defeat of Santa Anna by Sam Houston at San Jacinto; independent Republic of Texas established
1835-42	Second Seminole War: Seminole Indians driven out of Florida to west of the Mississippi
1837-40	Texas recognized as independent by the United States, France, and Britain
1842-43	Beginning of migration to Oregon along the Oregon Trail
1842-44	John C. Frémont explores the West
1845	Texas admitted to the United States
1846	War breaks out between Mexico and the United States
	Oregon treaty with Britain gives United States the Pacific Northwest south of the 49th parallel
	Bear Flag revolt by Anglos in California: Americans seize California
1847	Wars between settlers and Indians in the Pacific Northwest begin
	Mormons under Brigham Young settle in the Salt Lake Valley
	Kearny seizes New Mexico
	Treaty of New Granada gives the United States a right of way across the Isthmus of Panama
	Winfield Scott lands at Vera Cruz and advances into Mexico: capture of Mexico City
1848	Gold discovered in California
	Treaty of Guadalupe Hidalgo
1848-49	The California gold rush: 100,000 Americans come to California
	Frémont explores a railroad route across the Rockies
1850	Clayton-Bulwer Treaty: Britain and the United States agree not to obtain exclusive control over a canal through the Panama isthmus
1851	Filibustering expeditions against Cuba
	Plains Indians agree to a "settlement" at Fort Laramie
1853	The Gadsden Purchase

4

Expansion and Imperialism

The Importance of Manifest Destiny

Expansion and imperialism came to be "bad" words in the mid-twentieth century. For some Americans they were objectionable even in the mid-nineteenth century. Yet during the period 1825–50, Americans devoted vast amounts of energy to winning the West by pioneering, settling, conquest, and last but not least by a mass migration called the *gold rush*. Those who supported expansion argued that some nation or other would in the end take over the West. Russia, Mexico, and Britain were all possible rivals of the United States. The power that occupied the West first would rule it for centuries to come. Surely that power *ought* to be the United States! A writer in 1845 summed up the popular feeling by speaking of

the fulfilment of our manifest destiny to overspread the continent allotted by Providence for the free development of our yearly multiplying millions.[1]

- What do you think of the notion of America's manifest destiny? Would you have supported the idea in 1845?

- Political scientists sometimes speak of *power vacuums*. What does *power*

[1]From *The United States Magazine and Democratic Review*, July–August 1845. Quoted in Richard B. Morris, *An Encyclopedia of American History* (New York: Harper and Row, 1965), p. 193.

vacuum mean? Was there a power vacuum west of the Louisiana Territory c. 1830? Explain.

- As you read on, think of these questions:
  1. What other policies could American leaders have adopted?
  2. Why did certain groups in the United States object to expansionist policies?
  3. Why did potential rival countries give way to the United States?
  4. What did manifest destiny look like to Indians, black slaves, Mexicans, Cubans, and Canadians?
  5. What technological factors made the expansion possible? (Consider transportation, communication, industry, weapons such as the Colt revolver and the Winchester rifle.)

- It used to be fashionable to try to identify the *aggressor* in an international conflict. As you read about the acquisition of Texas, Oregon, New Mexico, Arizona, and California, see if you can identify the aggressor. Is it easy or difficult? Explain.

- Look at the "Chronology of Manifest Destiny" on page C-68. In how many different places was expansion taking place 1825–50? How would you describe the events? Were they part of a big imperialistic plan? How did the Monroe Doctrine relate to United States expansion?

► Look at the map on page C-6. Check the territories gained by the United States between 1845 and 1853.

The Golden West: California

Well to the south of the Oregon Country, a thin belt of Spanish civilization extended along the Pacific coast from San Diego to San Francisco. Between 1769 and 1823, Franciscan friars—encouraged by the Spanish government—had established 21 missions in Upper California (the present state of California). The churches and other buildings of those missions still stand, surrounded sometimes by modern cities. Gathering the Indian folk of California at these centers, the Franciscans offered them Christian teaching and instructed them in agriculture, animal husbandry, and crafts.

Up from Mexico came settlers of Spanish stock, who created vast ranches in California. After the Mexican Revolution, California was annexed to Mexico, and the missions fell into decay. The Mexican government was not popular with the Californians, and communication with Mexico City was difficult. Until the 1840's, California remained one of the most remote and most peaceful regions of the world.

Ships from Massachusetts began to sell goods in Californian ports in the 1820's. Some American traders and sailors took up residence in the province. The land route to California from the Mississippi and the Missouri was more difficult than either the Santa Fe Trail or the Oregon Trail, but American hunters came over the mountains in 1826. Some 15 years later a considerable overland immigration of Americans commenced. Among the newcomers was John Sutter, an American citizen of Swiss birth, who in 1839 built a

fort (still standing) in the Sacramento Valley. Sutter became an official under the Mexican government, maintained armed forces at his private expense, and grew rich. It was on his lands, in 1848, that gold was discovered. Meanwhile, until 1846, the new settlers carved out farms and trading posts in old California.

● The Franciscan missions changed the Indians' way of life. When the friars were expelled by the Mexican government, and the missions sold, the Indian converts scattered and returned to their old way of life. The Mexican government had thought it was benefiting the Indians by *secularizing* the missions. Can you think of arguments in favor of the survival of the missions? Why did both Spanish and Mexican governments intend that the missions should be only temporary?

★ Old California before 1847 has been called "a lotos-land society." What is meant by this? Would you have preferred to live in California about 1825, or in New York City at that time? Why?

★ Find out about the lifework of Father Junípero Serra.

Until nearly the end of the period 1825–50, American connections with New Mexico, Oregon, and California did not result in the transplanting of American political institutions to those regions. But things went otherwise in Texas.

Texas: The Lone Star Republic

About 1822, the spreading plains of Texas, the northernmost region of Mexico, were inhabited by wandering bands of Indians. Early in the nineteenth century,

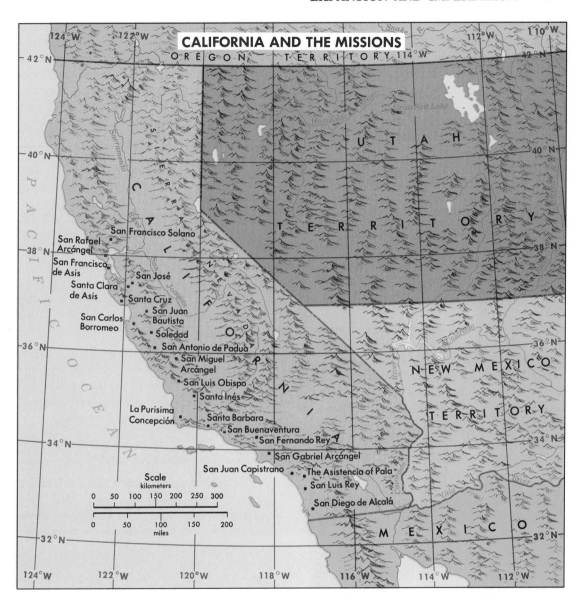

CALIFORNIA AND THE MISSIONS

the American government had asserted some claim to Texas, but had agreed to abandon that claim when Spain ceded Florida to the United States in 1819. Yet it was less difficult to reach Texas, from Missouri or Louisiana, than it was to penetrate to Sante Fe, Astoria, or the Californian capital of Monterey.

Eastern Texas was a good country for raising cotton. So into Texas there began to move United States citizens, who obtained Spanish citizenship—and Mexican citizenship, after the Mexican Revolution. They were given large grants of land, in part because the government at Mexico City hoped they would restrain the Texan Indians. By 1830, there were some twenty thousand Americans with a thousand Negro slaves, settled in Texas, chiefly in the neighborhood of Austin.

These vigorous Texas settlers did not long remain content under Mexican rule. They objected to Mexican import duties that made it difficult to import American goods. They demanded that the Mexican government lift its prohibition on the importing of more black slaves. They declared that the Mexican provincial government at Coahuila, far to the south, did not represent them; still less did they feel sympathy with the Mexican central government at Mexico City. Mexico, torn by civil struggles, had a weak government at best, and often the Texans found that government corrupt. These Anglo-Texans thought their land titles were insecure. Most of them were Protestants, while the Mexicans were Catholics. More important still, in culture and political beliefs they were people of the United States, not of Mexico.

This smouldering resentment took fire in 1836. The Americans in Texas, allied with a number of Mexican-Texans, rose against the Mexican government. The dictator Santa Anna marched against them. At the Alamo, a former mission near the town of San Antonio, Santa Anna surrounded and killed nearly 200 Texans—Anglos and Mexicans—who fought to the last man. Among the dead were Colonel James Bowie (after whom the frontier weapon called the *Bowie knife* was named), and the celebrated David Crockett—frontiersman, humorist, and former member of Congress. Santa Anna's troops killed 450 more Texan rebels at Goliad, a month later.

Santa Anna's triumph was brief. At the battle of San Jacinto, a few weeks later, the Mexican forces were destroyed by the Texan army, commanded by Sam Houston. Then the Texans declared their independence and established the Republic of Texas, the *Lone Star State*.

Texas soon was recognized as an independent country by the United States, Britain, France, and Belgium. Many Americans wanted Texas to join the Union. However, if Texas were to become one of the United States, it would enter as a slave state. Many Northerners were therefore opposed to the admission of Texas. Moreover, the annexation of Texas in 1836 would have brought on war with Mexico, and even President Jackson, stern old soldier though he was, would not venture so far.

● Did the government of the United States act justly and prudently in recognizing the independence of Texas? Why or why not? Did the Texans have a right to break away from Mexico? If Hawaii should demand independence from the United States today, would seceding Hawaiians offer arguments similar to those of the Texans in the 1830's? How about Puerto Rico?

★ Find out something about Davy Crockett, whose autobiography (probably dictated or authorized by him) was published in 1834, and has been a popular book ever since.

Sectionalism Versus Expansion

With the independence of Texas, the sectional rivalry between the free Northern states and the Southern slave states became a factor in the imperialistic policy of the United States.

● Why was westward expansion complicated by sectional rivalry? How had the problem been settled—at least temporarily—by the Missouri Compromise of 1820?

● Why were Southerners especially eager to add slave states to the Union?

In 1825 it was uncertain whether most of the West beyond the Mississippi ever would be divided into states and admitted to the Union. If the West should

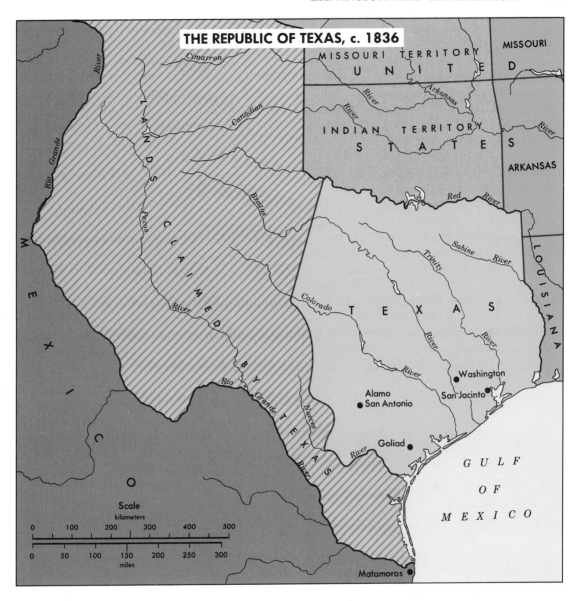

THE REPUBLIC OF TEXAS, c. 1836

become part of the United States, and the Missouri Compromise held good, about half the new states would be slave, and half of those states free. It was certain that eventually Florida Territory would become a state, which would add two senators to the South's voting bloc. It was probable that eventually Wisconsin and Michigan territories would become states, which would add four senators to the North's voting bloc. The Southerners would need

only one more slave state—Arkansas Territory, perhaps—to maintain the balance in the Senate. Beyond that, no one knew what future admission of new states might do to Henry Clay's Missouri Compromise.

For 15 years after the Missouri Compromise the question of admitting "free" states or "slave" states did not arise. In 1836, however, Texas wished to join the Union as a slave state. President Jackson, a man from Tennessee, had no sympathy for Northern Abolitionists. Yet opposition to slavery was so intense among many Northerners, by that time, that Jackson gave no support to the Lone Star State's application. Indeed, he even postponed formal diplomatic recognition of the Republic of Texas until the very day he left office. If Texas had been admitted to the Union in 1836, once more the balance of free and slave states in the Senate would have been upset.

True, another slave state, Arkansas, was admitted to the Union in 1836, under the provisions of the Missouri Compromise. It was balanced by the free state of Michigan, admitted a few months later. The territories of Wisconsin, Minnesota, and Iowa now were filling up with white settlers, and soon would apply for statehood. (Only 60,000 resident citizens of the United States were required for a territory to apply for statehood.) It began to appear that the free states soon would outnumber the slave states, after all.

For eight years after the admission of Michigan, in 1837, no new states were admitted to the Union. Meanwhile, North and South drew farther apart in spirit, as the slavery question grew increasingly menacing. The antislavery people in the North and the champions of the plantation economy in the South were equally determined that their own faction must win the West.

● The Missouri Compromise chose a parallel of latitude as the basis for determining whether a new state should be "free" or "slave." Was this a practical solution to the dispute? Why was the parallel of 36° 30' selected? Can you think of some other principle upon which a compromise might have been arranged?

The siege of the Alamo, March 6, 1836

Why would slave labor have been unprofitable in Michigan or Iowa?

Manifest Destiny Carries the Day

Before 1846, the expansion of the United States across the Mississippi had occurred mainly by chance rather than by plan. About the time when James K. Polk was elected president, in 1844, however, the idea of manifest destiny took hold of many Americans' imagination. Some men advocated forceful expansion of American power all the way to the Pacific, so that the United States would be secure against all enemies. Others, chiefly in the South, saw in swift westward expansion an opportunity to extend slavery. Such extension would ward off Northern threats of abolition. Yet other advocates of expansion saw in the Far West the possibility of great gains in commerce and good land.

President Polk and other expansionists seized upon the notion of manifest destiny. According to this theory, it was the will of God that the citizens of the United States should spread American institutions — American freedom, American government, American culture, American economic methods — from sea to sea, and perhaps farther afield. Some leading men talked of annexing Cuba, of expanding the United States right down to the Isthmus of Panama, and of persuading or compelling Canada to enter the Union. An influential advocate of such grand designs was the historian George Bancroft, whose extremely popular *History of the United States* (the first volume was published in 1834) expressed the conviction that divine providence had ordained the rise and growth of the United States. Bancroft was an antislavery Democrat, but he became secretary of the navy in Polk's cabinet.

If the United States were to expand rapidly, who would have to yield territory to the American Republic? The Indians would, of course; that was taken for granted. Sturdier opposition might be expected from the British government, where the Oregon Country was concerned; and from the Mexican government, where Texas, New Mexico, and California were in question.

Since the War of 1812, the United States had not fought any powerful enemy. During the War of 1812, the government at Washington had hoped to annex Canada — but had been badly defeated there, the Canadians not wishing to be forced into the Union. Now many Americans felt ready for a bigger struggle. The poet Walt Whitman, learning of discontent in Yucatán (a southern province of Mexico) during 1846, wrote an editorial entitled "More Stars for the Spangled Banner," in which he argued that Yucatán "won't need a long coaxing to join the United States." Such enthusiasts for "the American Idea" believed that the American way of life should be extended as far as possible.

- The word *destiny* implies that some superhuman power has determined how a person or a nation must act — and that therefore it would be foolish to try to act differently. Do you believe that you can act in your own life very much as you wish — or that you have a "destiny" that makes certain things possible or impossible for you?

- Do you think that great nations have destinies? Is "destiny" the same thing as the will of God? Is the United States of our day destined to accomplish some great mission?

- During the Civil War, a clergyman told President Lincoln that "God is on our side." Lincoln replied that he didn't know that; he only hoped that we (the Union cause) were on His side. Is there some danger in believing that "God is on *our* side"?

The Sectional Line-Up 1837

Free States	Slave States
Pennsylvania 1787	Delaware 1787
New Jersey 1787	Georgia 1788
Connecticut 1788	Maryland 1788
Massachusetts 1788	South Carolina 1788
New Hampshire 1788	Virginia 1788
New York 1788	North Carolina 1789
Rhode Island 1790	Kentucky 1792
Vermont 1791	Tennessee 1796
Ohio 1803	Louisiana 1812
Indiana 1816	Mississippi 1817
Illinois 1818	Alabama 1819
Maine 1820	Missouri 1821
Michigan 1837	Arkansas 1836
13 Free States	13 Slave States

The Oregon Dispute

Almost simultaneously, President Polk was involved in difficulties with Mexico and Britain. Although Polk desired to expand America's frontiers on a large scale, he really did not desire war with either power—and certainly not with both at once. So he found it prudent to settle with Britain first.

Ever since 1818, American citizens and British subjects had been jointly occupying the Oregon Country. As American settlement and American commercial investment in Oregon increased, Americans who believed in manifest destiny declared that the whole of the Oregon Country must come under the authority of the United States. They took up the slogan "Fifty-Four Forty or Fight"—meaning that unless the British government would cede the whole of Oregon to the United States, right up to 54° 40′ latitude, then Americans would take Oregon by force.

However, Polk had no intention of going to war with the British Empire, by far the greatest power in the world. Nor did the British desire to fight for so distant a region: for one thing, the Oregon fur trade already was declining. By diplomacy, America and Britain settled upon a division of Oregon at the forty-ninth parallel—except that the whole of Vancouver Island remained in Canada. Out of America's southern half of the Oregon Country, new states could be created—and presumably they would be "free" states. This treaty with Britain was signed on June 15, 1846.

● Why wasn't the British government concerned about Britain's "manifest destiny" in North America? Would Britain have found it more difficult to fight for Oregon than the American government would have found it? What regions of the world may have seemed more important to the British government in about 1846?

★ What nation controlled the Pacific coast north of 54° 40′?

Texas Joins the United States

Meanwhile many Americans wanted desperately to admit Texas to the Union. Many others opposed the move. John Quincy Adams, speaking for the anti-slavery people, said that the South only wanted Texas as "a pen to cram more slaves in." However, in 1844 President Tyler arranged a treaty with Texas. Under this treaty Texas was to become a part of the United States. Treaties must be ratified by two-thirds of the Senate (Article II, Section 2, paragraph 2 of the Constitution of the United States). In fact, however, the treaty did not even obtain a majority. The Senate rejected it 35 to 16.

The Democratic candidate in 1844, James K. Polk, ran on an expansionist platform. Not only did he promise to seize Oregon, he also swore to "re-annex" Texas. He won the election by a fractional majority, but outgoing President Tyler claimed Polk's victory was a popular mandate for expansion. He proposed that Congress admit Texas by a *joint resolution.* This was done. The resolution passed 27–25 in the Senate, and 132–76 in the House. The people of Texas ratified the decision, and the Lone Star State joined the Union in December 1845.

● Why was a joint resolution for annexation much easier to pass than a treaty? Might a strict constructionist object to such a method as unconstitutional? Explain.

Quarrel with Mexico

Texas had been at war with Mexico ever since 1835. It was a war of skirmishes and raids, mainly in the area between the Rio Grande and Nueces River. (See the map of Texas in 1836, on page C-73.) Texas claimed that its southern boundary was the Rio Grande. Mexico denied that claim, and rejected Texas's claim to independence. Texas also claimed land to the west, including most of New Mexico with its trading center at Santa Fe. Thus, when the United States annexed Texas, it took over Texas's conflict with the Republic of Mexico.

The United States had another quarrel with Mexico. A number of Americans had been hurt or had lost their property in revolutionary upheavals in Mexico. The Mexican government had failed to pay compensation to these American citizens.

When war seemed almost inevitable, President Polk tried to buy California and New Mexico from Mexico for $30 million. Included in the deal were the Rio Grande boundary for Texas. The United States also offered to pay compensation to Americans who had suffered losses in Mexico. The Mexican government would have nothing to do with this offer.

In the meantime, it was evident that Mexican politics were very unstable. One government was overthrown early in 1846. General Paredes then seized power. Paredes himself was later overthrown.

President Polk was well aware that a large number of Americans opposed both the annexation of Texas and the prospect of war with Mexico. He moved cautiously, seeking to compel the Mexican army to attack first. American forces under Zachary Taylor advanced into the disputed area on the northern bank of the Rio Grande. American cannons pointed at the Mexican city of Matamoros. In May, 1846, the Mexicans at last crossed the river and attacked. "American blood had been spilled upon American soil."

● Do you think that Mexico was the aggressor? Explain.

● Can you justify President Polk's policy? How?

★ The war with Mexico was not an all-out war to conquer Mexico. It was a *limited* war. What is a limited war? What were the objectives of the United States? What were the objectives of Mexico? What general rules will the commanders in a limited war tend to follow? Will they aim at massive battles designed to destroy the enemy? Why or why not?

● Why does a limited war tend to divide public opinion on the home front? Does a desperate all-out war in which both sides aim at crushing the enemy also divide public opinion? Why or why not?

● Do you think the weakness and instability of Mexican government encouraged the American government to make war? Explain.

● Look at the map on page C-81. What strategy was used by the United States?

Many European observers thought that Mexico could win a defensive war on its own territory. The Mexicans thought so, too. In the northern United States, especially in New England, the war with Mexico was unpopular, especially because it was looked upon as a war to extend the Cotton Kingdom of slavery. The writer Henry David Thoreau went to jail (briefly) rather than pay taxes that might be used to support the war. Within the United States, opinion about the necessity and justice of the Mexican War was as badly divided as American opinion about the war in Vietnam in the late 1960's and early 1970's.

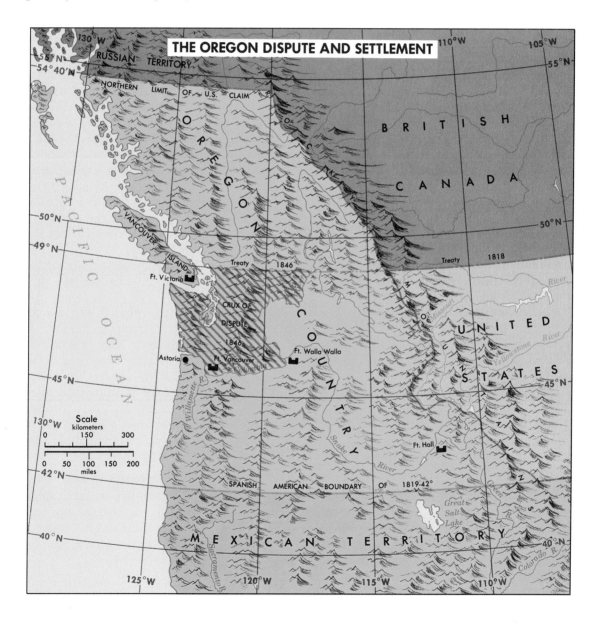

THE OREGON DISPUTE AND SETTLEMENT

The Course of the War

The government of the United States at first hesitated about invading Mexico. Then the decision was made to attack on several fronts. The Americans were helped and encouraged by the selfishness and corruption of many Mexican leaders. Those Mexicans who were interested in politics were divided into rival groups. Catholics were opposed by anti-Catholics. The mass of the Mexican people were apathetic. A Mexican history text remarks:

A national conscience was lacking, and the foreign war was regarded with indifference, since the vast majority of the population was illiterate and did not know the meaning of the word Fatherland.[2]

Despite these disadvantages, many Mexican soldiers fought with great, though hopeless, courage.

The United States took advantage of Mexico's internal troubles. The United States government enabled General Santa Anna (the dictator who was defeated by Houston at San Jacinto) to return from exile in Cuba. The United States apparently hoped that Santa Anna would seize power and make a peace favorable to the Americans. Santa Anna did indeed seize power in Mexico, but he continued the war. His military leadership, however, was extraordinarily poor, so the American gamble in enabling him to return did in fact pay off.

The American strategy took the form of three major land campaigns, a seaborne invasion, and a naval blockade. The ports of Mexico, both east and west, were blockaded by the American navy. California and New Mexico were conquered by Colonel Stephen Watts Kearny, who marched from the Missouri River to Santa Fe, San Diego, and Los Angeles. Kearny was assisted by Colonel Frémont's expedition in northern California and by the revolt of Anglo-American settlers in California.

Meanwhile, it was decided to invade the heart of Mexico. United States General Zachary Taylor struck south and west across the Rio Grande, gaining victories at considerable expense in human lives (American and Mexican). Taylor did not penetrate Mexico south of Monterrey and Buena Vista in the Province of Nuevo León. Another force, led by Colonel Alexander W. Doniphan struck south from New Mexico and captured Chihuahua.

Still the Mexicans refused to surrender, although they had lost control of California, New Mexico, and Texas, and had been defeated in their northern provinces. To compel surrender, a seaborne invasion under veteran commander General Winfield Scott was planned. Its aim was to force the Mexican government to recognize the hopelessness of further resistance. Scott was a meticulous planner and a general who believed that battles should be won with a minimum loss of life. His attitude is well summed up by some words in a message to Santa Anna after the latter had been defeated at Churubusco (August 20, 1847):

Too much blood has already been shed in this unnatural war between the two great republics of this continent.[3]

● How does Winfield Scott's point of view reflect the strategic and tactical aspects of limited war?

On March 9, 1847, Scott landed his forces at Vera Cruz. His operation is said to be a model of *amphibious warfare*. After taking Vera Cruz by siege, he took the

---

[2]C. Gonzalez Blackaller y L. Guevara Ramirez, *Síntesis de Historia de México* (Mexico, D. F., Editorial Herrero, S. A., 1968), p. 318. Translated by the authors of the present book.

[3]Quoted in Russell F. Weigley, *The American Way of War: A History of United States Military Strategy and Policy* (New York: Macmillan, 1973), p. 76.

risky course of marching inland across 200 miles of rough, mountainous country to the capital city. He could hardly have dared to risk such a campaign with less than 10,000 men, had the Mexicans been organized for guerrilla war to harass his line of communication. As it was, Scott advanced steadily, winning a number of battles, and captured Mexico City on September 13–14, 1847. Santa Anna made a last attempt to fight, at Guadalupe Hidalgo. He then resigned and fled to Jamaica. A provisional government signed the Treaty of Guadalupe Hidalgo on February 2, 1848.

The Peace Treaties

Some members of Polk's cabinet wished to conquer all of Mexico and annex the country permanently to the United States. But by the Treaty of Guadalupe Hidalgo, the American government settled for less. Mexico surrendered New Mexico and California to the United States, and agreed that the Rio Grande should be the southern boundary of Texas. Mexico, in fact, surrendered more than half of its territory to the United States. The United States paid Mexico $15 million for the ceding of those territories. Then American

President James K. Polk

General Winfield Scott

General Zachary Taylor

THE MEXICAN WAR

troops were withdrawn from Mexico proper.

The Treaty of Guadalupe Hidalgo also included stipulations as to the future of Mexicans living in the ceded territories. They were to retain all their personal and landed property. Their civil, political, and religious rights were also guaranteed. Although Mexico lost half its territory, it lost only one per cent of its population. Some 80,000 Mexicans stayed in the ceded territories and sooner or later became citi-

zens of the United States. The Treaty did not mention the Indians in the territories, although they had been citizens under Mexican law. In practice, both Mexican Americans and Indians suffered much discrimination in the newly acquired lands. Culture conflicts and discrimination still persist at the present day.[4]

[4]See, for example, Matt S. Meier and Feliciano Rivera, *The Chicanos: A History of Mexican Americans* (New York: Hill and Wang, 1972), pp. 69–73 and 74ff.

● Could the Mexican War have been avoided? If both parties had desired earnestly to prevent the war, what compromises might have been made? Is there such a thing as a "just war"? Under what circumstances might a war be considered just?

● Why was the Mexican government less willing to compromise than was the British government during this period?

The Triumph of "Manifest Destiny"

Now the United States controlled the whole of the Atlantic coast from northern Maine to the Florida Keys, the whole of the Pacific coast from Puget Sound to the borders of Baja California—and everything in between. If indeed it had been the American Republic's destiny to rule from sea to sea, that destiny had been accomplished—with much help from American rifles. The only remaining struggle would be with Indian tribes. That fight continued, at intervals, for half a century longer, but there was no prospect that the American government could lose it.

The Mormons

Now the empty interior of the American Republic beyond the Mississippi filled up with surprising speed. Even while the Mexican War was in progress, a new kind of pioneer had crossed the Rockies and settled around the basin of the Great Salt Lake and in the valleys of Utah. These pioneers were a religious community, the members of the Church of Christ of the Latter-day Saints, commonly called the Mormons. More than 1,500 of them reached the Great Salt Lake in September, 1847, and by 1850 more than 11,000 Mormons were there.

Although the Mormons were Chris-

The storming of Chapultepec, a fortified hill commanding the roads into Mexico City on September 13, 1847

tians, they had suffered persecution in New York, Illinois, Ohio, Missouri, and elsewhere. The sect had been founded by Joseph Smith, at Palmyra, New York, only two decades earlier. They differed from other Christian bodies in that they had their own new prophetic teaching, *The Book of Mormon,* which Smith declared had been revealed to him divinely. What caused a greater scandal, the Mormon leaders approved of "plural marriage" — that is, a husband might have several wives. They were eager to convert others to their faith. This also roused hostility often. Also their economic practices seemed un-American to many: the Mormons believed in an economic community founded on religious principles, and their church maintained storehouses to help those who were in need. Joseph Smith was lynched by a mob, and the Mormons were driven out of one refuge after another — some of them even withdrawing to Mexico.

Brigham Young, the Mormons' new leader, determined that they could live in peace only if they should live outside the boundaries of any existing state, in some territory where Mormons would form the majority of the population. The settlement of Utah was his solution. Despite terrible hardships, Mormons made their way to the Great Salt Lake country. Many came from England. Some actually pushed handcarts across the prairies and mountains.

The Mormons named their country Deseret. Some of them pushed north into Idaho, and others crossed the deserts of Nevada into southern California. It seemed as if they were creating an empire, for Deseret (nominally Mexican territory until the Treaty of Guadalupe Hidalgo) included what now is Utah, Arizona, and Nevada, and portions of New Mexico, Idaho, Colorado, Wyoming, and California.

In 1850, Brigham Young and other Mormon leaders tried to have Deseret ad-

mitted as one of the United States. However, the Mormon settlements seemed to Congress too strange for statehood. The territory claimed by the Mormons was immense; it was said that non-Mormons (whom the Mormons called "Gentiles") were unsafe there. Moreover, the Mormon institution of polygamy was condemned. Deseret, refused statehood, remained almost an independent nation until after the Civil War, when Brigham Young was compelled to submit to the authority of the government at Washington.

★ The Latter-day Saints, or Mormons, are said to have professed the first "new American religion" — not counting, of course, the Indian religions. Look up information about Joseph Smith and *The Book of Mormon.* What does *The Book of Mormon* teach about the origin of the American Indians?

★ Is there something especially American about the Mormon faith? If so, why did the Mormons soon make a great many converts in Britain and other countries? Have the Mormons changed any of their principles or practices since their early settlement in Utah?

● The Mormons succeeded very well in commerce and agriculture. How may their moral principles of close cooperation within their religious community have helped them economically?

New States, 1845–48

Although Deseret (which did not tolerate slavery) was not admitted as a state, four other states joined the Union during, or just after, the Mexican War: Florida and Texas (both slave states) in 1845; Iowa and Wisconsin (free states) in 1846 and 1848. Thus the balance in the Senate between free and slave states was maintained. By 1848, it stood at 15 free states and 15 slave. But California was about to be admitted as a state, and that upset the balance.

Effects of the Gold Rush of 1849

Into California came a breed of immigrants very different from those who settled Deseret. Near Sutter's Fort, where the city of Sacramento now stands, gold was discovered early in 1848. Within a few months, news of the mineral wealth of California had spread round the world. By ship or along the California Trail, gold-hunters rushed to sleepy old California. Within two years, a hundred thousand men had arrived to pan or dig for gold not only from the Eastern United States and the Western territories, but from many countries, even China. The "Forty-Niners," bursting upon the little towns and Spanish ranches in 1849, tore Californian society apart.

Law and order virtually collapsed. Many of the Spanish-speaking inhabitants and the American citizens who had settled earlier lost their lands because of vague title-deeds. Even the powerful John Sutter was ruined by gold-hunters who took over his lands. Robbers and desperate characters roved the countryside and the towns. *Vigilante committees* hanged as many of them as they could catch, usually without trial in a court of law.

To save California from anarchy, it was necessary to organize the territory as a state. President Zachary Taylor, elected in 1848, asked that both California and New Mexico prepare state constitutions and enter the Union. The proposed constitutions of California and New Mexico both forbade slavery.

● Why was military government in California, once the gold rush began, incompetent in maintaining order? (A European statesman said

The Mormon's first tabernacle at Salt Lake City, 1858

These people are panning for gold in a stream in California in 1849

once, "You can do everything with bayonets—except sit upon them.") How was it that a state government, elected under a state constitution, could better control a population that had multiplied several times in two years?

Another Uneasy Compromise on the Question of Slavery

The enormous question before the Thirty-First Congress, in 1850, was how to preserve the Union, threatened anew by the problem of slavery versus freedom in Western territories. From the summer of 1846 onward, many Northerners had tried to persuade Congress to adopt the *Wilmot Proviso*, which would have required that slavery be prohibited in all this land annexed to the United States. Southerners replied that because the Constitution recognized slavery, the "peculiar institution" could not be forbidden in the new terri-

tories. If slaveowners should wish to settle there (as many of them did), they must be permitted to take their slaves with them.

★ Look at Amendment V of the Constitution. If slaves were legitimate property, could Congress deprive persons of that property when they moved into the territories of the United States? Why or why not? This is a tricky question. What does *due process of law* mean?

★ Suppose Congress had voted to *pay compensation* to slaveowners for the loss of their slaves. Would this have satisfied the stipulation in the Fifth Amendment? What factors probably prevented Congress from considering this solution?

Early in 1850, Congress began to consider the applications of California and New Mexico to join the Union. Both territories had drawn up constitutions that prohibited slavery. Furious Southerners in Congress resolved to prevent the admitting of these two territories to statehood. If the "free" states were to outnumber permanently the "slave" states, would not the day soon arrive when the federal government might take away the Negroes from the Southern planters, ruin the economy of the South, and disrupt its society?

Already many Northern congressmen were ready to abolish the slave trade in the District of Columbia; indeed, they would have liked to abolish slavery altogether in the District. If California and New Mexico were to enter the Union, cried Senator Robert Toombs, of Georgia, then his state and other states might go out.

● Why was the slave trade and slavery in the District of Columbia especially annoying to Northern congressmen? Why was it so important—from another point of view—to Southerners?

At this point, Henry Clay came forward with a compromise, as he had done admirably on other occasions. Senator Clay proposed that California be admitted as a free state; that the rest of the regions acquired from Mexico be given territorial governments, without any prohibition of slavery there for the present; that other disputes be resolved by concessions on either side. Senator John C. Calhoun sternly opposed the compromise; Senator Daniel Webster ringingly supported it.

After long disputes, Congress adopted the chief features of Clay's proposals. California came in as a free state; New Mexico and Utah became territories where slavery was· tolerated; the slave trade was abolished in the District of Columbia; and Congress provided a stronger federal law to require free state authorities to return fugitive slaves to their Southern masters. Reluctantly, both North and South accepted an arrangement that satisfied neither section of the country.

Advocates of the Compromise of 1850 declared that this was the final solution of the slavery dispute. They were mis-

The Compromise of 1850

1. California admitted as a free state

2. New Mexico and Utah to be territories where slavery was permitted

3. Texas was paid $10 million to give up its claims to New Mexico

4. Stricter federal fugitive slave law, including fines of $1,000 for helping a fugitive slave or preventing his arrest

5. Abolition of the slave trade in the District of Columbia

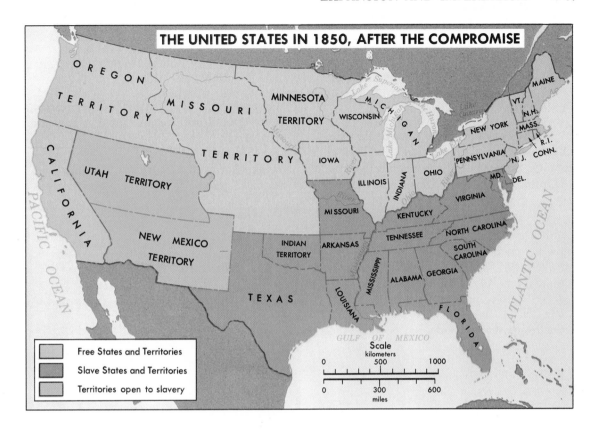

THE UNITED STATES IN 1850, AFTER THE COMPROMISE

Free States and Territories

Slave States and Territories

Territories open to slavery

Scale
kilometers
0   500   1000

0   300   600
miles

taken, for within four years the sinister question rose again. It was not to be settled until 1865.

The End of an Era

With the Great Compromise, comes the end of the "Middle Period" or "Silver Age" of American history. Some of its principal actors—Madison, Monroe, Randolph, Marshall, Jackson, J. Q. Adams, Crawford—had died years earlier. Calhoun died a few months before the compromise was agreed upon; Clay and Webster died about two years later. A brilliant generation was ending.

The census of 1850 showed that there were more than 23 million people living in the United States—more than 3 million of them slaves. Already there were nearly 10,000 miles of railroad in operation, and the rails were transforming the West far faster than wagon trains could have done. Manifest destiny, as expressed in America's continental expansion, had been realized. The United States now was a great power.

Conclusion

An Unsettled People

The census of 1850 showed that the country was big in population as well as in territory. Some 23 million people lived in the United States. More than 13 million of them were in "free" states and territories, fewer than 10 million in "slave" states and territories.

Some 2,241,000 of them were foreign-born. More than 3 million were slaves. There were about 434,000 free Ne-

Chronology of American History, 1825-50			
EVENTS IN THE UNITED STATES			EVENTS IN THE REST OF THE WORLD
John Quincy Adams, 6th president	1825		
John Caldwell Calhoun, vice-president			
Erie Canal completed			
Controversy over the Panama Congress	1826		
Changed method in electing presidential electors	1828		
The Tariff of Abominations			
Presidential election			
Andrew Jackson, 7th president	1829		
Calhoun again vice-president			
Webster-Hayne Debate	1830	1830	Revolution in Paris
Jackson vetoes the Maysville Road			Polish Revolution put down by Russia
Joseph Smith starts Mormon Church			France takes Algiers
Garrison starts *The Liberator*	1831		
Nat Turner's Rebellion in Virginia			
Worcester v. Georgia			
Nullification in South Carolina			
Jackson vetoes the Bank Charter Bill			
Jackson reelected president	1832	1832	Reform Bill in Britain
Martin Van Buren, vice-president			
Treasury withdraws funds from the Bank of the United States	1833	1833	Santa Anna president of Mexico
Rise of the Whig Party	1834	1834	Abolition of slavery in British colonies
A year of riots and violence	1835		
Specie Circular	1836	1836	Independent Republic of Texas
Roger B. Taney, Chief Justice of the U.S.			
Martin Van Buren, 8th president	1837	1837	Victoria queen of Great Britain and Ireland
Richard M. Johnson, vice-president			Rebellion in Canada
Economic panic and depression			
Gag rule against Abolition petitions in Congress			
Tensions with Britain	1838		

groes. Nobody knew quite how many Indians there were—but surely several hundred thousand of them. The most populous region of the Republic still was the Middle Atlantic section. On the Pacific coast, only 106,000 people were found by the census-takers.

Most of these 23 million Americans had great expectations, but also they experienced grave discontents. The strain of national expansion had left its mark upon them. Bitter sectional hostilities roused tempers and prejudices, despite the im-

mense gains of territory by both Northerners and Southerners. Although the national income had increased tremendously during the past quarter of a century, that gain had not brought contentment.

A recent social historian, Rowland Berthoff, describes the conflict between material prosperity and social confusion among American citizens about the middle of the nineteenth century:

A people who made economic progress their pre-eminent value could discern only dimly the fundamental but far less salutary upheaval that

Liberty party	1839		
Independent Treasury Act	1840		
Whig candidate, William Henry Harrison, wins presidential election			
Harrison, 9th president, dies. John Tyler becomes 10th president.	1841	1841	British war against China (the "Opium War")
Repeal of Independent Treasury Act		1841-44	Dictatorship of Santa Anna in Mexico
Creole Case	1842		
Webster-Ashburton Treaty			
Dorr Rebellion in Rhode Island			
Native American party founded (later the Know-Nothing party)	1843		
Oregon Dispute	1844		
Presidential election: James K. Polk defeats Henry Clay			
Polk, 11th president	1845		
George M. Dallas, vice-president			
Annexation of Texas			
Oregon settlement with Britain	1846	1846	Repeal of Corn Laws in Britain
War with Mexico begins			Famine in Ireland
Wilmot Proviso			Santa Anna returns, as ruler of Mexico
Invasion of Vera Cruz	1847	1847	Independent Republic of Liberia
Capture of Mexico City			
Gold discovered in California	1848	1848	Year of revolutions in Europe
Treaty of Guadalupe Hidalgo			Italian war of independence
First Women's Rights Convention			
Zachary Taylor, 12th president	1849		
California applies for statehood	1850		
Compromise of 1850			
Clayton-Bulwer Treaty			
Death of Taylor; Millard Fillmore, 13th president			

was undermining the primary institutions of their social order. They were preoccupied with the tasks of economic growth: opening up the land and the other resources of the continent; gathering an industrial working class from Europe and rural America into new urban centers; applying a new technology to commercial transportation and industrial production. There was a further problem that Americans did not yet recognize . . . the consequent slackening of the strands that had bound the old institutions of society together seemed quite acceptable, even desirable. It was one thing, however, to free the individual enterpriser for the material development of the country. It proved quite another for the individual to get along without the non-economic values of life that had been embedded in the old social order.[1]

Under the strain of national expansion, many Americans had lost their roots. America in 1850 was muscular and prosperous, but often the family, the community, the church, and the class to which people belonged had been weakened. Almost everything west of the Mississippi seemed new and raw. Even in the East, the new industrialism had disturbed or destroyed traditional ties between persons. A recent writer, Hannah Arendt, remarked that "the rootless are always violent." Ten years later, violence exploded tremendously in the United States.

● Alexis de Tocqueville, in the 1830's, had written that the great majority of Americans were materialistic; but that their customs and moral habits, or "mores," kept their democratic society free, reasonably honest, and reasonably peaceful. Are Americans less materialistic nowadays? What does "materialism" mean? Are the Soviet Union and Communist China materialistic?

● Why should rapid territorial and economic expansion partially break down the old loyalties to family, community, church, and class? Has this happened again to the United States in the twentieth century?

Reform and Violence

There was, it is true, a certain amount of internal violence in the United States in the 1830's and 1840's. It was not to be compared with the violence of the 1850's and 1860's, but it was a symptom of restlessness and insecurity. Slavery was an institutionalized system of violence by which large numbers of people were deprived of liberty. It gave rise to violent episodes in various parts of the country.

The growing cities, too, were often torn by violence. Between 1830 and 1850 there were at least 28 serious riots in Baltimore, Philadelphia, New York, Boston, and Cincinnati. These were sparked by many varied social and political factors. There were labor riots resulting from the discontent of workers. There were riots stemming from elections. There were riots against Abolitionists, Negroes, and Catholics. One result of these upheavals was the introduction of municipal police forces to replace the antiquated system of constables and watchmen.[2]

Vigilante movements occurred in various parts of the United States. These were organized movements by groups determined to take the law into their own hands — usually because the laws were inadequately enforced by public officials. Students of the topic have identified vigilante movements in Indiana, Illinois, Georgia, Mississippi, Alabama, and Arkansas in the 1830's. In the 1840's vigilantes were on the prowl in Iowa, Texas, Illinois, Kentucky, and California.[3]

---

[1] Rowland Berthoff, *An Unsettled People: Social Order and Disorder in American History* (New York: 1971), p. 174.

[2] See Hugh Davis Graham and Ted Robert Gurr, *The History of Violence in America* (New York: Bantam, 1969), pp. 53–54, and 60.

[3] *Ibid.*, p. 157.

The expressions of the new politics and social movements were not usually violent, however. Democracy, urbanization, and social dislocation brought many ardent movements for reform. The treatment of the deaf, the blind, and the mentally ill was improved. Efforts were made to reduce the amount of drunkenness in society: in 13 states alcohol was prohibited by 1857. Labor unions began to appear, and socialistic ideas were imported from Europe. The movement for women's rights was launched in 1848.

★ Find out about some of the reformers of the period: Dorothea Dix and the reform of the treatment of the mentally ill; Elizabeth Cady Stanton and Lucretia Mott and the women's rights movement; Elihu Burritt and the peace movement; Neal Dow and the prohibition movement; Henry Thoreau and civil disobedience.

★ Find out about some of the religious reform movements: William Miller and the Adventists; Ann Lee and the Shakers; Charles G. Finney and revivalism.

★ What is *utopian socialism?* Find out about the French socialist Charles Fourier. Find out about some of America's utopian communities: Brook Farm in Massachusetts, New Harmony in Indiana, Oneida in New York, Ripon in Wisconsin. Were these communities successful?

★ One problem created by industry was child labor. Americans were slow to do anything about this. Find out about the Massachusetts child labor law of 1836. Was it effective? When did the national government succeed in forbidding child labor in interstate commerce?

The Antislavery Movement

The most famous reform movement of the period was the antislavery movement. This movement had many separate elements. Probably most Northerners and Northwesterners were opposed to slavery, but few were prepared to agitate for its abolition in the slave states. They opposed its extension into the territories, however. Many were also willing to petition for its abolition, or for the abolition of the slave trade, in the District of Columbia.

The petitions for abolishing the slave trade in the District of Columbia led to some disturbing results. These petitions began to be sent to Congress in 1835. They infuriated Southerners in Congress. In 1836 the House of Representatives voted to refuse to accept any petitions related to slavery. This rule was not repealed until 1844. Northerners called it the *gag rule.* They regarded it as a fundamental attack on freedom of speech. Southerners also refused to allow antislavery materials to be sent by the mails in the Southern states. These actions convinced many moderate men and women that Southern slave interests were the enemies of constitutional liberty. Thus the so-called fire-eaters of the South managed to drive into a growing antislavery coalition many Northerners who had originally no intention of interfering with the "peculiar institution."

In the course of time many such persons began to feel sympathy for the radical Abolitionists. These Abolitionists were, for many years, only a handful of agitators. They were committed to the belief that slavery was a deadly sin. Some, like William Lloyd Garrison, thought that the free states should secede from the Union. Garrison even called the Constitution "a covenant with death and an agreement with hell." Such extreme views were almost as unpopular in the North as in the South. Abolitionists were persecuted and

Some Violent Episodes of the 1830's and 1840's (not including Indian Wars)

1831	Nat Turner's Rebellion
1834	Political riot in Baltimore
	Anti-Negro riot in Philadelphia
	Election riots in Philadelphia and New York
	Anti-Abolition riot in New York
	Anti-Catholic mob burns a convent in Boston
	Federal troops put down labor protest in Maryland
1835	Bank riot in Baltimore
	Anti-Negro riot in Philadelphia
	Anti-Abolition riot in New York
	Labor riot in New York
	Anti-Abolition mob ("Garrison mob") in Boston
1836	Two pro-slavery riots in Cincinnati
1837	Broad Street mob in Boston
	Food riot in New York
	Murder of Elijah Lovejoy by anti-Abolition mob in Illinois
1838	Anti-Abolitionist riot in Philadelphia
	Anti-Negro riot in Philadelphia
1840	Anti-railroad riot in Philadelphia
1842	Anti-Negro riot in Philadelphia
	Bank riots in Cincinnati
1843	Weavers' strike riot in Philadephia
1844	Two Anti-Catholic, anti-Irish riots in Philadelphia
1847	Firemen's riots in Baltimore
1848	Election riot in Baltimore
1849	Election and anti-Negro riots in Philadelphia
	Theatrical factions riot in New York

were often the targets of mob violence in the 1830's and early 1840's.

Gradually, however, attitudes changed. Southerners often seemed as extremist as the Abolitionists. The genera-tion that was coming into its own in the North in the 1850's was less and less willing to bow before the "slaveocracy." Twenty years of Abolitionist propaganda was bearing fruit. Twenty years of proslavery fire-eating had begun to create a hard core of antislavery feeling in the North.

- Do you think that Southern fire-eaters did their own cause more harm than good? Explain. What alternative strategies were open to them?

- Why were most Northerners opposed to the radical Abolitionists? What arguments in favor of radical agitation can you give? What were the arguments against such agitation?

- Why did Garrison call the Constitution "a covenant with death and an agreement with hell"? (The phrase comes from Isaiah 28:15.)

- The generation of 1825–50 had avoided, postponed, and compromised the issue of slavery. Why was it most unlikely that the generation of 1850–80 could continue this indecisive attitude?

Responses to the Challenges of 1825–50

The introduction to this section listed several powerful challenges that the American Republic began to confront about 1825. The people of the United States certainly responded to those challenges in a muscular way: some challenges they met adequately, but others they failed to confront successfully.

The challenges of national expansion, in general, had been met with courage, but sometimes without much imagination. The expansion itself had brought to the country a mood of hopefulness, despite sectional disputes and the worry of slavery. It seemed as if Americans could win almost anything they might want—territory, wealth, clever inventions, military success. The Americans seemed unbeatable—except by other Americans.

The challenge of democratic politics had been faced, at least for the time being, with some success. The "political revolution" of 1828, when the democratic Jacksonians had triumphed, had not torn American society apart, after all. Government might be less high-minded than it had been in the early decades of the Republic, but still the United States enjoyed a good measure of order, justice, and freedom. The extension of the franchise to nearly all white males had not resulted in mob rule.

The challenge of presidential powers had not upset the American political structure. No American president had tried to make himself a dictator, and Congress remained vigorous. In both Senate and House, able men continued to lead. No president since 1825 had been very imaginative, but all had been competent enough.

The challenge of a two-party system also had done little mischief. Most of the time, party leaders had been responsible men. Democrats and Whigs did not really hate each other—not even under the stress of sectional tensions—with a few exceptions. Election campaigns, by and large, had not grown more scandalous since 1828, and there was no widespread increase of political corruption.

The challenge of America's economic future had been dealt with successfully—if we are to measure success by material production. The incomes of nearly all classes and sections had increased famously over a quarter of a century. American technology had surpassed that of Europe, in many respects. The new cities might be ugly, yet immigrants from abroad seemed glad to settle in them. As yet, the rural pattern of life, Northern or Southern, was not much disturbed by the growth of industry and commerce. On the frontier and in the backwoods, strong men and women were clearing land, draining swamps, breaking the sod of the prairies—in the expectation that they and their children would make steady and swift progress. New inventions had made Northern and Western agriculture remarkably efficient.

The challenge of immigration had turned out to be less serious than some reflective people had expected. James Russell Lowell, some years later, regretted in his section of the country "the change from New England to New Ireland"—meaning that the New England states were being crowded with rough Irish immigrants. Yet most of the 2,241,000 foreign-born residents of the United States, in 1850, had adjusted surprisingly well to the American pattern of life. Some lived in city slums, but they were rising in the scale and sharing the general increase of American prosperity. Many of them soon became active in American politics—usually voting for Democratic candidates. There had occurred a few episodes of resentment and rebellion—most notably, the desertion of some American soldiers of Irish birth to the Mexican army during the Mexican War, because they had found themselves fighting against fellow Catholics.

The challenge of creating an American intellectual culture had not been ignored. American novelists, poets, essayists, and historians now were read everywhere in the Western civilized world. Distinctive American architectural styles, a wide variety of them, appeared even in the raw new states. Painting and sculpture found American patrons. In every Northern state, a beginning had been made toward the establishment of a free public school in every community—this under the influence of the educational reformer Horace Mann, secretary to the Massachusetts state board of education from 1837 to 1848. The South and the West were slower in such measures, but they made headway, too. Churches often founded and operated schools. Church-related colleges sprang up

in almost every state, and several important state universities were founded during this period.

The challenge of manifest destiny had been ended, for good or ill, by the acquiring of nearly all the territory which today makes up the midcontinental United States. Much of this had been taken by force, but the temptation to conquer the whole of Mexico had been rejected. With a swiftness that amazed Europeans and many citizens of the Eastern states, the Western territories organized themselves into states or at least found little difficulty in adapting American political patterns to their circumstances. The United States had no powerful enemies to confront in 1850. And, up to 1850, any major struggle with the Western Indians had been avoided—though fighting with the Plains Indians began the very next year.

To the grimmest challenge, slavery, there had come no adequate response by 1850. Slavery had not diminished in the lower South; indeed, it seemed to be expanding rapidly into much of the Southwest. Hopes for emancipating Negroes and settling them somewhere in Africa had been abandoned. Although the slave trade had been abolished in the District of Columbia, it continued in all the slave states. In the North, the Abolitionists were denouncing the South mercilessly; in the South the fire-eaters were equally reckless. No one in America had thought of a way to solve the riddle of slavery.

Sectionalism, the challenge to unity of the Republic, woke no more intelligent response. John C. Calhoun had proposed that the Union might be preserved by his doctrine of *concurrent majorities*. This doctrine proposed that the several sections of the United States should agree upon an amendment to the federal Constitution, which would provide that if any section should be treated unjustly, it might interpose its sectional authority against some federal statute or policy. But this proposal had got nowhere. It was an attempt to legalize nullification.

Controversy over tariffs had diminished, but the slavery question truly sounded now like "a fire bell in the night," as Jefferson had said long before. In June of 1850 a number of Southern leaders who feared the drift of antislavery opinion in the North and in Congress held a convention at Nashville, Tennessee. They condemned the Compromise of 1850, by which California had been admitted to the Union as a free state. At the Nashville convention, and at similar state conventions in Georgia, Mississippi, Alabama,

Some Intellectual Events, 1825-50

c1825	Greek revival in architecture under way
1826	James Fenimore Cooper's *The Last of the Mohicans*
1827	Massachusetts requires every town of 500 families to set up a high school
1830	Joseph Smith founds the Mormons
1833	Oberlin College: first coeducational college
1834	George Bancroft's *History of the United States* (Volume 1)
	Pennsylvania's Free School Act
1836	Ralph Waldo Emerson's *Nature* (beginning of New England Transcendentalism)
	Mount Holyoke: first permanent women's college
1837	Emerson's *The American Scholar*
	Horace Mann begins school reforms in Massachusetts
1838	John Greenleaf Whittier's *Poems Written During the Progress of the Abolition Question*
1840	Richard Henry Dana, Jr's., *Two Years Before the Mast*
	Edgar Allen Poe's *Tales of the Grotesque and Arabesque*
	Gothic revival in architecture begins
1843	William Hickley Prescott's *History of the Conquest of Mexico*
1846	Herman Melville's *Typee*
1847	Henry Wadsworth Longfellow's *Evangeline*
1848	James Russell Lowell's *Biglow Papers*
1849	Henry David Thoreau's *A Week on the Concord and Merrimack Rivers*
	Francis Parkman's *The California and Oregon Trail*
1850	Nathaniel Hawthorne's *The Scarlet Letter*

John C. Calhoun

and South Carolina, Southerners talked of possible secession from the Union—if Congress should treat the South unjustly.

Only in South Carolina, however, did the Southern sectionalists definitely reject the Compromise of 1850. The outbreak of civil war was thus postponed for another decade, for South Carolina could not stand alone against the national government. The cause of this moderation in 1850, North and South, seems to have been economic. The United States was so prosperous that year that neither Northern industrialists nor Southern planters desired to fight. Tariffs were low in 1850, American agricultural products were selling well abroad, and gold was pouring in from California. By November of 1850 the Southerners of the Nashville convention, or most of them, had decided to do nothing rash; they would accept the compromise.

Only a few years later, when territories in the Great Plains were ready for statehood, that Compromise of 1850 fell apart. Henry Clay, the Great Compromiser, was dead by then. No one else in the United States was able to suggest a plan to diminish the intensity of sectionalism. Young William H. Seward, an antislavery senator from New York, declared in 1850 that soon the Negroes would be emancipated, and that "there will be no disunion and no secession." His prediction proved wrong.

★ Look up information about Calhoun's ideas of *concurrent majorities* and *interposition*. Why had Calhoun given up the concept of *nullification* of federal statutes by a single state?

● If Americans had met most of their national challenges fairly well by 1850, why could they not avert the coming of the Civil War little more than ten years later? How was it that the people of the United States were so resourceful in meeting large challenges, when they had little central direction—no national boards of planning, no national university, and not even any departments of research in their political parties?

★ Did Russia, a centralized country also expanding rapidly during this period of history, succeed in meeting its challenges better than did the United States?

The Americans of 1850 had more land than they knew what to do with, more thriving industry than any other country except Britain, more gold than they ever had dreamed of. They seemed to lack for nothing—except roots. Everything in America seemed bigger than life. Within a few years, the Americans found themselves in the biggest war since the days of Napoleon.

Unit Six
Secession, Civil War, Reconstruction (1850–1880)

THE TWENTY-SECOND NATIONAL
ANTI-SLAVERY BAZAAR,
TO BE HELD IN BOSTON, MASS., DURING THE CHRISTMAS WEEK OF 1855.

This annual effort, having for its end the Abolition of American Slavery, has been so long before the eyes of the community, that we feel prolonged explanation in respect to it unnecessary. A very simple statement will be sufficient for our purpose.

Convinced as we are that slavery is a sin and a crime every where and under all circumstances, that all complicity or connivance with it implies moral guilt just in proportion to the extent of the sanction given, that consequently all political, and especially all religious fellowship with such a system of abominations is eminently criminal and dangerous, it is our endeavor to promulgate these sentiments, so far as may be in

(left) A newspaper announcement of an "Anti-Slavery Bazaar" (above right) A slave auction

Introduction
The Challenges of the Civil War Generation

What was life in the United States like in the 1850's? America was a prosperous land, though it had depressions every few years. Thousands of immigrants from Ireland and Germany were pouring in year after year. These were the years of the Industrial Revolution, when towns rapidly grew into cities. If a man could not find work or afford to purchase land in the East, there was always the Great West—expanded by America's victory in the Mexican War. Lands were being cleared, railroads constructed, towns founded: America was on the move.

Yet in the 1850's the United States, for all its expansive prosperity, was a troubled land. Serious problems had cropped up in the earlier decades of the century, and many of them had *not* been solved.

★ Review your knowledge of the period 1825–50. How would you define the main problems of the period? Which problems still threatened trouble in the 1850's? Consider: sectionalism, slavery, race relations, the westward movement, organizing new territories and states, relations between Indians and white settlers, women's rights.

The problems persisted through the 1850's. In 1861 they came to a head. In that year, the American Civil War (or War Between the States) broke out. It lasted over four years. More than 600,000 persons were killed (or died as a direct result of the war), and at least 400,000 were wounded or maimed.

After the war was over, many of the troublesome problems of the *ante-bellum* (prewar) period seemed solved. Yet some remained, and many new ones emerged.

● Which earlier problems might be solved by the victory of the Union? Which would probably persist? What new problems might emerge?

The period 1850–80 can thus conveniently be divided into three subperiods. First, from 1850 to 1860, certain divisive issues grew sharper and more dangerous, in spite of efforts to find *compromise solutions*. Second, from 1861 to 1865, a bitter war was fought. Third, from 1865 to 1880, Americans sought to clean up the mess left by the war and to face further challenges of territorial and economic expansion.

Some Historical Questions To Think About

The period 1850 to 1880 was as crucial as any in the history of the United States. Consequently, historians have devoted a great deal of research to this period. Historians have also disagreed about nearly every important issue. Was the Civil War inevitable? Was the real issue slavery? Could the South have won? Was the Union (Northern) policy after the

Immigration, 1820-80 (in thousands)

	Great Britain	Ireland	N-W Europe	Germany	Poland and Central Europe	Russia and Eastern Europe	Italy	Other Southern Europe	China	Canada	Mexico*	Other America	All other countries	Total all countries†
1820-30	27	54	13	7	—	—	—	3	—	2	5	5	33	152
1831-40	76	207	54	152	—	—	2	3	—	14	7	13	70	599
1841-50	267	781	110	435	—	—	2	3	—	42	3*	17	53	1,713
1851-60	424	914	142	952	1	—	9	10	41	59	3	12	29	2,598
1861-70	607	436	201	787	9	2	12	9	64	154	2	10	18	2,315
1871-80	548	437	367	718	86	40	56	20	123	384	5	15	—	2,813

*80,000 Mexicans joined the U.S.A. in 1848 by the Treaty of Guadalupe Hidalgo.
†The total figures include immigrants from some places not shown.

war correct? Were the black people in the South betrayed? Was the treatment the Indians suffered necessary?

▶ Look at the chart on page C-103. Use this as a check list for reference as you pursue your studies.

The Challenges Faced by the Generation of 1850–80

The questions listed in the chart are the questions historians ask. Historians have the advantage of hindsight.

Another way of looking at the period is through the eyes of the people at the time. What challenges were faced by ordinary people and their leaders—white and black, Northern, Southern, or Western, immigrant and native American? What choices had they? How did they make their decisions? Did they really have a choice, or was the course of events more or less inevitable?

The Challenge of Identity

A central challenge faced by nearly all Americans might be called the challenge of *identity* or of *loyalty*. Should a person regard himself first and foremost as an American, owing loyalty to the United States? Or should he think of himself as a Northerner, Southerner, or Westerner, with sectional loyalties? Or should he think of himself as an Ohioan or a Virginian or a Marylander, whose prime loyalty was to his state and his *state's rights?*

● How did Afro Americans, Hispanic Americans, Chinese Americans, and American Indians think of themselves? Were they Americans or aliens?

● Look at the map on page C-104. How many states were there? Which would you classify as Southern, Northern, Western, and

Middle (or Border) states? Which areas came into the United States as a result of the Mexican War and Gadsden Purchase? What section or sections would they fall in?

● How might *natural environment* and *historical experience* lead to differing and conflicting interests and needs in different sections? Give examples of such differing interests.

● How might these differing interests impede the efficiency and policies of the national government? Consider especially legislative decisions in the House of Representatives and the Senate.

● The Founding Fathers constructed a solution to the problem of states' rights versus the necessary powers of the national government. What was that solution? How might it contribute to dangerous conflict or deadlock in the period 1850–60?

● Does sectionalism exist in the United States today?

★ Have other nations, during their early years of political development, experienced difficulties brought about by sectionalism? Give examples.

★ What parallels might be drawn between the American experiences of the 1850's and Canadian politics today?

By the 1850's the concept of one nation consisting of several sections and many semi-sovereign states began to give

Historical Disputes over the Period 1850-80

1. Why did the Civil War occur and could it have been avoided?

2. Alternatively: What were the main issues in the Civil War: Growth of conflicting interests between sections? Slavery? Conflicting ideas of nationality? Conflicting interpretations of the Constitution? Others?

3. When secession occurred, what choices had the new president, Abraham Lincoln? How important were his personal decisions? Why did he make them?

4. What were the strategies and tactics of the North and South? Why were they chosen? Were they sound?

5. What part did the personalities of leaders play in the war and in the Reconstruction period? Consider: Lincoln, McClellan, Grant, Sherman, Douglass, Garrison, Sumner, Stevens, and Johnson in the North; Davis, Lee, and Jackson in the South.

6. What part was played in and during the war by ethnic groups such as black Americans, German Americans, American Indians, Irish Americans, and Mexican Americans in the new territories?

7. What policies were open to the victorious North in dealing with the South after 1865? Which were tried and why? How successful were they?

8. How can one assess the major lasting results of the war and Reconstruction?

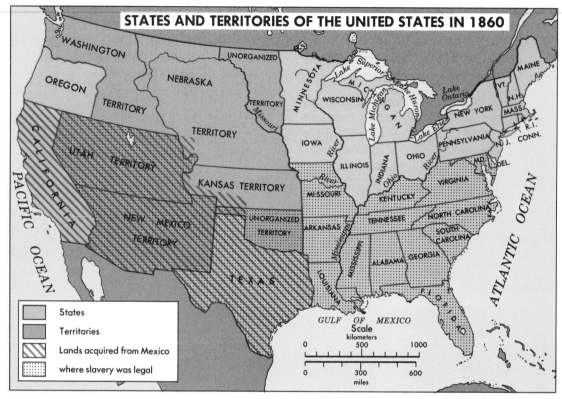

STATES AND TERRITORIES OF THE UNITED STATES IN 1860

Legend:
- States
- Territories
- Lands acquired from Mexico
- where slavery was legal

Scale
kilometers
0   500   1000

0   300   600
miles

way to another notion. That notion was that instead of one United States of America there might be two or more independent nations. Particularly in the South there was a growing feeling that the slave states could prosper more if they were not politically united with the North.

● What economic factors might make Southerners feel that union with the North hindered their prosperity? Consider conflicting interests over *tariff policy* and other matters.

● In controversies between the South and the North where would the Western states tend to line up?

★ In Europe the question of nationalism and national independence was acute during the mid-nineteenth century. What examples of national independence movements in Europe can you mention? How would this general concern with national iden-

tity affect Americans? How would immigrants from Ireland and Germany be likely to regard the issue of American nationalism? How might European nations react to a claim of national independence on the part of a section of the United States?

★ The American Revolution was a *secession*—an assertion of national independence. How might this successful example affect Americans in the 1850's?

The Challenge of Slavery and Race Relations

Were sectional differences too great for peaceful compromise? Was there some factor that made them peculiarly explosive? There *was* such a factor: the institution of black slavery in Southern states. What to do about this "peculiar institution" presented a grim dilemma. Furthermore, the more white Americans discussed the dilemma, the more bitter and extreme became their differences.

The issue had at least three aspects: the moral, the social or racial, and the economic. The *moral* aspect was this: in nearly every part of Western civilization there was growing condemnation of slavery. Since the 1820's, slavery had been abolished in the British and French empires and in most of Latin America. The African slave trade was regarded as piracy by most Western nations, including the United States. Slavery or serfdom did survive in parts of Asia and Africa, in Brazil, Cuba, Russia, Poland, Portugal, and in the Southern states of the United States.

★ The antislavery movement in the United States and Europe was part of a larger movement called *humanitarianism*. What was the nature of the humanitarian movement? What ideas and emotions inspired it? What other examples of humanitarian agitation can you give in the United States and in Europe?

★ How was slavery ended in the British Empire? In Haiti? In Mexico? In Puerto Rico?

★ Can you defend slavery on moral grounds? What was the proslavery argument? When did it become popular in the South?

● Imagine yourself a slaveowner or living in a slaveowning society. How would moralizing criticisms and denunciations of slavery from outside affect you? What would you say in reply to someone who told you that slaveholding was a sin? How would the moral aspect of the slavery issue increase irrational hostility between the slave states and the free states in America?

● Imagine yourself a slave. Would you try to run away to the North? Would you try to plan a revolt? Explain. How might you know that there was an antislavery movement? What would be your chances of successfully running away if you were a slave in Alabama? In Missouri? Explain.

The second (*social* and *racial*) and third (*economic*) aspects of slavery were much more important to Southerners than they were to Northerners. Consider the social and racial aspect. In the Southern slaveholding states, there were in 1860 about 4 million Negro slaves and about 8 million whites. Only about 400,000 whites actually owned slaves. Yet most Southern whites supported slavery. They could not imagine how so many blacks could live and work alongside the white population unless the blacks were held down by the cruel discipline of slavery. *Racial prejudice* — the feeling that Negroes were inferior and incapable of looking after themselves — was widespread among Southern whites. For most Southern whites, therefore, slavery was a means of social control, and therefore "morally justified." Even on the moral aspect of slavery Southerners thought they were right!

● Why would the average Southern white be deeply afraid of the sudden freeing of the slaves?

● Why did "poor whites" prefer to see the Negroes kept in slavery?

★ What slave revolts had occurred in the United States? Had there been slave revolts in other parts of the world? How could such revolts be used in arguments justifying slavery?

● Explain the relation between slavery and racial prejudice. Does racial prejudice exist in the United States today? Can you give any evidence of it?

The economic argument for slavery was mainly to the effect that the economic prosperity of the South depended on slave labor. The poor whites and others who did not own slaves also felt that their standard of living would fall if they had to compete with free black workers. Moreover, slaves were property. A man who owned 20 slaves had as much as $12,000 to $16,000 invested in his work force. Who would compensate him if the slaves were emancipated? Some would ask: *Ought* he to be compensated?

● Most Abolitionists had no sympathy for the loss a slaveowner would suffer if his slaves were freed. What is your opinion on the matter?

● Imagine yourself a Negro slave, a free black, a Southern white slaveholder, a poor Southern white, a Northern factory worker, or a farmer in Ohio. What position would you have taken on slavery? What way out of the dilemma would you have suggested or chosen?

What form did the slavery controversy take? Except for a small number of Abolitionists, white Americans — North, South, and West — agreed that the national government could not and should not interfere with slavery inside the slave states. Most Americans, however, agreed in 1850 that the national government could make laws for the *territories* of the United States. Most Americans also agreed with the Missouri Compromise of 1820, which prohibited slavery north of the line 36° 30'. Consequently, the proslavery and antislavery forces tended to concentrate their attention on the territories and new states. Proslavery people were eager to add territory in the South; they also wanted to ensure that slavery was introduced in all territory

south of the Missouri Compromise line. Some Southerners were beginning to argue that the Missouri Compromise was unconstitutional. They said Congress could not exclude slavery from *any* territory. Antislavery people, meanwhile, became increasingly nervous about the extension of slavery beyond the existing slave states. One additional bone of contention was the problem of *fugitive slaves.* More and more Northerners refused to help Southerners to recover slaves who had escaped north of the Mason and Dixon line. These issues — slavery in the territories and fugitive slaves — became dangerously explosive in the 1850's.

★ What did the Constitution say about fugitive slaves? (See Article IV, Section 2, clause 3.) About slaves in general? (Article I, Section 2, clause 3, and Section 9, clause 1.)

The Challenge of Civil War and the Challenges of Reconstruction

In later pages we shall look at the challenges of decision in the year 1860 and in the 1860's and 1870's. Deciding how to vote in the presidential election of 1860 must have been a deadly serious matter. So must deciding to secede and deciding how to react to secession. Then came the many challenges of war itself and, finally, the challenges of the post-bellum period.

★ List some of the probable challenges you perceive in the war and postwar periods.

What Can We Learn from the Generation of 1850–80?

Through our examination of the ways in which the men and women of the Civil War and Reconstruction periods met the great challenges of their time, we can learn not only about the causes and effects of that war, but also about the problems of loyalty, patriotism, and race relations faced by our own generation in the United States and by other peoples of the world.

In his second Inaugural Address, Abraham Lincoln said:

With malice toward none; with charity for all; with firmness in the right, as God gives us to see the right, let us strive on to finish the work we are in; to bind up the nation's wounds; to care for him who shall have borne the battle, and for his widow and his orphan—to do all which may achieve and cherish a just and lasting peace among ourselves and with all nations.

Today, men and women are still attempting to meet Lincoln's final challenge.

A cotton scene at Meridian, Mississippi, 1880. (Left) Weighing cotton; (Middle) Loading cotton on a train; (Bottom left) A cotton farmer waiting for a buyer; (Bottom right) Pressing cotton into bales

Eva and Uncle Tom in "Uncle Tom's Cabin"

John Brown's last moments as he is led out to be hung

Proslavery men shot down Free-Soilers at the massacre on the Marais Des Cygnes River in Kansas on May 19, 1858

1
A Decade of Crises, 1850-60

Between 1850 and 1860 a series of clashes occurred between the proslavery and antislavery sections. Each clash left tempers frayed. The culminating effect was the rise of a new, Northern party dedicated to preventing the further extension of slavery. When the new party captured the presidency in 1860, the proslavery forces felt pushed into secession and rebellion. Let us look at the major crises of the fateful decade.

The Missouri Compromise Begins To Fail

The great congressional debate over slavery took place in 1819–20, when Henry Clay was Speaker of the House of Representatives. The result of the debate was the Missouri Compromise, which lasted for 30 years. It was a fairly simple plan: Of the territory acquired by the Louisiana Purchase, all land north of 36° 30′ (except the state of Missouri) would henceforth be free territory; all land south would be slave.

For about 30 years after the Missouri Compromise, Congress took great pains to see that whenever a free territory petitioned for statehood there would be a slave state received into the Union at the same time.

● Look at the chart on page C-110. Why did Congress, especially the Senate, place such emphasis on the balance between slave and free states?

★ Investigate the Ostend Manifesto. Which section wanted the United States to annex Cuba? Why?

● Look at the map on page C-111, showing territorial gains from the Mexican War. What might the proslavery group hope for in these new territories?

● The people of the territory of California wanted their territory to enter the Union as a *single free state*. How would Southern politicians feel about the proposal?

★ Why had the population of California increased so rapidly in 1848–50?

★ Investigate the history of San Francisco. How was the native Spanish-speaking population affected by changes that took place when the city became a part of the United States in 1848?

A New Compromise in 1850

When California demanded statehood, Southerners felt that the balance of free state and slave state representation for Congress was threatened. Henry Clay worked out one more compromise.

States of the Union and Dates of Admission, up to the Civil War

(Admission to 1820)

	Free		Slave
1787	Pennsylvania	1787	Delaware
1787	New Jersey	1788	Georgia
1788	Connecticut	1788	Maryland
1788	Massachusetts	1788	South Carolina
1788	New Hampshire	1788	Virginia
1788	New York	1789	North Carolina
1790	Rhode Island	1792	Kentucky
1791	Vermont	1796	Tennessee
1803	Ohio	1812	Louisiana
1816	Indiana	1817	Mississippi
1818	Illinois	1819	Alabama

(Admission 1820 to 1861)

	Free		Slave
1820	Maine	1821	Missouri
1837	Michigan	1836	Arkansas
1846	Iowa	1845	Florida
1848	Wisconsin	1845	Texas
1850	California		
1858	Minnesota		
1859	Oregon		
1861	Kansas		

● Look at the box on page C-112. Which provisions might please the North? Which the South? Which were good for blacks? Which were not?

● Why were the Northerners not particularly concerned that Utah might become a slave territory? Recall the religion of the Latter-day Saints, or Mormons, who began settling the region in 1847.

In spite of Clay's efforts, the Compromise of 1850 was a failure. As is so often the case, something that tries to satisfy everyone satisfies no one. Each side felt that it had given up too much. Many Southerners doubted that the Southwest had sufficient land suitable for cotton. They felt that the cotton economy was the very basis of the entire American economy. On the other side, many Northerners could not accept the new Fugitive Slave Law. By its provisions, a slaveowner, pursuing a runaway black and capturing him, needed only to swear that the escapee was his slave. Citizens were forbidden to aid the runaway. In response to the Fugitive Slave Law, 13 Northern states passed Personal Liberty Laws, which were meant to *nullify* the national law. These laws further antagonized Southerners, who came to feel that the North had reneged on the compromise.

● What was there about the cultivation of cotton that caused the Southerners to need more and more land for expansion?

★ Were Southerners correct in their belief that cotton could not be grown in Arizona and New Mexico?

★ What was the government's policy toward the Indians living in the region acquired from Mexico?

★ What was the *Underground Railroad?* How was it related to the Fugitive Slave Law?

★ Why did the publication of *Uncle Tom's Cabin* in 1852 create so much uproar in both the North and the South?

★ How did the Personal Liberty Laws of various Northern states nullify the Fugitive Slave Law? Did this nullification differ from South Carolina's nullification of the tariff during President Jackson's term of office?

The Kansas-Nebraska Act, 1854

Although faulty, the Compromise of 1850 created some semblance of peace for about four years; in 1854, an ambitious

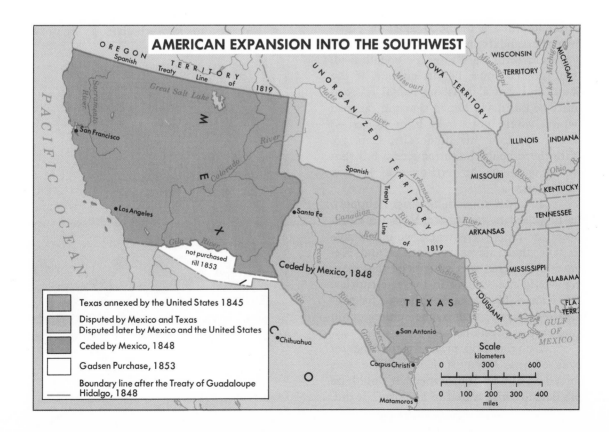

AMERICAN EXPANSION INTO THE SOUTHWEST

Texas annexed by the United States 1845
Disputed by Mexico and Texas
Disputed later by Mexico and the United States
Ceded by Mexico, 1848
Gadsden Purchase, 1853
Boundary line after the Treaty of Guadaloupe Hidalgo, 1848

The Compromise of 1850

1. California admitted as a free state

2. New Mexico and Utah to be territories where slavery was permitted

3. Texas was paid $10 million to give up its claims to New Mexico

4. Stricter federal fugitive slave law, including fines of $1,000 for helping a fugitive slave or preventing his arrest

5. Abolition of the slave trade in the District of Columbia

politician's proposal destroyed the status quo. As a result, much blood was shed over the slavery issue.

The politician was Stephen Douglas, a senator from Illinois. Douglas tried and failed to be the Democratic presidential candidate in 1852. He believed that westward settlement must be encouraged, that Indians must be driven out of the West, and that a transcontinental railroad must be built. He hoped that the railroad (which would need help from Congress) would run from his home city, Chicago. With these goals, he introduced a bill that would open up the territories of Kansas and Nebraska.

In order to gain Southern support, he proposed to repeal the Missouri Compromise. Thus slaveowners would be able to take their slaves to Kansas and Nebraska. Douglas was convinced that slavery would not survive in these territories. His Kansas-Nebraska Act allowed for *popular sovereignty;* that is, the settlers could vote on the question.

Douglas said privately that the repeal of the Missouri Compromise was forced on him by Southerners. It would, he predicted, "raise a hell of a storm." It did.

The Kansas-Nebraska Act was passed. In the North it roused great anger. Douglas was a clever politician, but the Kansas-Nebraska Act destroyed his own hopes of becoming president and brought calamity to the nation.

● Why would the opening of Kansas and Nebraska help prepare the way for a northern route for the transcontinental railroad?

★ The Gadsden Purchase (1853) had opened a southern route for a transcontinental railroad from New Orleans to San Diego. Find the Gadsden Purchase on the map on page C-104. Why might Douglas be in a hurry to pass the Kansas-Nebraska Act?

★ What does *popular sovereignty* mean? Why was popular sovereignty in the territories also called *squatter sovereignty?* Do you think it was a mistake for Congress to give up its power to say whether a territory

Dred Scott

Stephen Douglas was such a powerful politician that he was called the "Little Giant." His schemes for bypassing the sectional conflict by devices like squatter sovereignty did more harm than good to the country and to his own career

should be slave or free? Why or why not? What might happen if both slaveowners and Free-Soilers rushed to settle Kansas and form a majority there? Douglas said privately that he felt sure that in the end Free-Soilers would win. Even if he was right, did the act show good judgment?

Bleeding Kansas: The Rise of a New Party

Kansas was torn apart by a local civil war. Hundreds of men died and millions of dollars worth of property was destroyed. The principle of popular sovereignty encouraged all sorts of graft and violence. Proslavery men came into the territory to raid. Sometimes they came merely to vote. Free-Soil settlers came to stay. Many came prepared to fight. Each side hoped to gain a majority in the election that would decide whether Kansas should be free or slave.

★ What were "Beecher's Bibles"? What was the Massachusetts Emigrant Aid Society?

★ What were the *Pottawatomie* and *Marais des Cygnes massacres?*

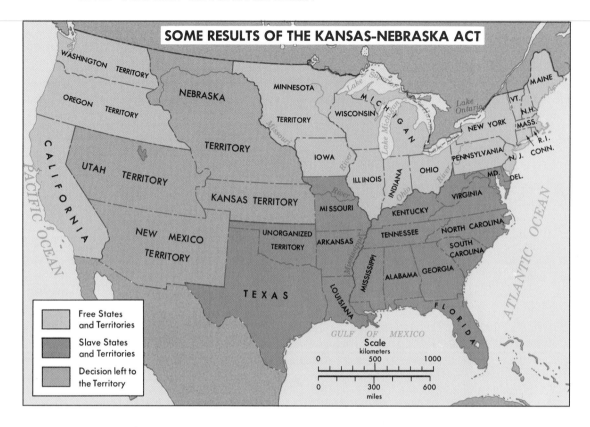

SOME RESULTS OF THE KANSAS-NEBRASKA ACT

Legend:
- Free States and Territories
- Slave States and Territories
- Decision left to the Territory

★ Investigate the life and career of John Brown. What part did he play in "Bleeding Kansas"?

The bloodshed in Kansas helped to create a new political party. The new party demanded that slavery must be kept out of *all* new territories. Founded at Ripon, Wisconsin, the *Republican party* soon replaced the Whig party, which split along sectional lines. Northern Whigs generally joined the new Republican party, while Southern Whigs became Democrats. Most Republicans were not Abolitionists; and unlike earlier *third parties*, the Republicans had views on many general issues as well as on the special topic of slavery. To some Southerners, however, that "stinking, putrid, Abolition party" was the next-to-last straw. It took only the election of its presidential candidate—Abraham Lincoln—in 1860 to "break the camel's back."

● The long-time tradition of the South being politically *solid Democrat* dates from the 1860 election. What are the objections to the domination of a section by one powerful political party?

★ During the 1850's another "third party," the *Know-Nothings*, made its appearance. Who were they? How might their success have prevented the outbreak of the Civil War? How did they disappear by 1860?

★ The Republican party is the only third party to replace a major party in American political history. Why is it so difficult for a third party to succeed? How does the system of the electoral college contribute to third-party failures?

● In 1856 James Buchanan, Democratic candidate, won the presidency. Look at the table showing election results. How close did the result come to being a purely *sectional* one?

The Dred Scott Decision, 1857

In a time of growing crisis, James Buchanan provided no positive leadership. Two days after he became president another crisis occurred. It came from the Supreme Court's *Dred Scott* decision.

In 1834, Dr. John Emerson, an army surgeon, purchased a slave in Missouri. Soon after, Emerson and his black house servant, Dred Scott, moved to the free state of Illinois. After living there briefly, the Emerson household moved to the free territory of Wisconsin. In 1838, the family returned to Missouri. Soon after, Dr. Emerson died.

About eight years later, Dred Scott—with the assistance of Abolitionist attorneys—sued Emerson's widow for his freedom. He claimed that his residence in a free state and a free territory had rendered him a free man. The defendant, Emerson's widow, really wanted the plaintiff to win, for she had married a Massachusetts Abolitionist, and had become an Abolitionist herself. Thus she desired to have her slave legally freed so as to set a *precedent*. A precedent is a guide to be used by other courts when deciding similar cases. In 1852, however, the highest court in Missouri decided that Dred Scott, by returning to a slave state, had become a slave once more.

● What *precedent* did Dr. Emerson's widow hope to see established by the court?

● In your opinion, does there appear to be anything faulty in the logic of the decision handed down in 1852?

At length Dred Scott's lawyers brought the case to the United States Supreme Court, which rendered a decision on March 6, 1857. The majority opinion was delivered by Chief Justice Roger Taney. Taney was a Marylander, appointed by President Jackson.

The Court first decided that Dred Scott was not a United States citizen. According to Taney, the writers of the Constitution never intended that Negroes should become citizens. Therefore, Dred Scott could not sue in federal courts. He was a person without *civil rights*. Taney might have stopped at his point, but he seems to have thought that he could help settle the whole slavery controversy. So he further declared that the Missouri Compromise of 1820 was unconstitutional. Congress could not prohibit slavery in the territories. The Court noted that in American law slaves were property. Therefore Congress, by prohibiting slavery in some areas, had deprived many citizens of their right to property. Thus Congress had violated the Fifth Amendment, which forbids

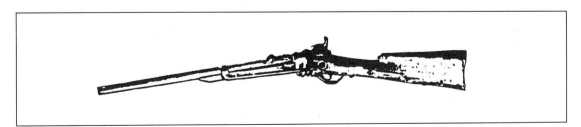

"Beecher's Bible"

depriving any person of property without due process of law.

● What would be the effect of the *Dred Scott* decision on blacks in the free states?

● What could antislavery groups do about this decision? How can a decision of the Supreme Court be altered?

★ Many scholars consider that much of the *Dred Scott* decision was an *obiter dictum*. What is meant by this phrase? What weight does it carry as far as future decisions are concerned?

★ Chief Justice Taney had freed his own slaves long before this decision. Yet his decision was *racist*. It was also *political*. Explain.

★ What were the *Lincoln-Douglas debates* of 1858? What was their significance in connection with the *Dred Scott* decision?

★ In 1859, there was another crisis. Find out about John Brown's raid on Harpers Ferry.

The Election of 1860

In 1860 came a presidential election. Its results started a chain reaction that brought on the Civil War. How did this come about?

First of all, the Democratic party *split on sectional lines*. A nominating convention in Charleston, South Carolina, was deadlocked. Another convention was held in Baltimore. It nominated Stephen Douglas of Illinois. Most Southerners now hated Douglas's idea of popular sovereignty in the territories. They claimed that the *Dred Scott* decision entitled a slave-owner to take his slaves to *any* territory.

The Southern Democrats broke away from the party. They nominated John C. Breckinridge of Tennessee.

The Republicans met in Chicago.

The Presidential Election, 1856

	Popular Vote	Electoral Vote
James Buchanan (Dem.)	1,838,000	174
John C. Frémont (Rep.)	1,341,000	114
Millard Fillmore (Know-Nothing)	875,000	8

How the states went:

19 for Buchanan:	All Southern states, and Delaware, Missouri, Illinois, Indiana, and Pennsylvania
11 for Frémont:	All New England, New York, Ohio, Michigan, Iowa, and Wisconsin
1 for Fillmore:	Maryland

President James Buchanan

Harriet Beecher Stowe

Harriet Tubman

They soon realized that the nomination of their foremost member, William Seward of New York—a well-known antislavery leader—would precipitate violence and possibly a civil war. They therefore nominated an apparently more moderate politician, Abraham Lincoln of Illinois. Lincoln was not an Abolitionist; like most Republicans, he simply opposed the extension of slavery into more territories. Even so, many Southerners predicted that if Lincoln were elected—or any Republican for that matter—the South would secede from the Union.

Finally, a group was hastily formed whose main objective was the preservation of the Union at all costs. Recognizing that the Democratic split between Douglas and Breckinridge would insure Lincoln's victory, the new party—called the National Constitutional Union party—came out in favor of permitting slavery in all territories. Its candidate was John Bell of Tennessee.

● Look at the table on page C-119. Answer these questions.

1. Was Lincoln a purely *sectional* candidate?
2. How was it possible for Douglas, with a large popular vote, to have so small an electoral vote?
3. Was Lincoln a *minority president?* Explain.
4. What is interesting about the votes of Virginia, Kentucky, Tennessee, and Missouri?

★ What other minority presidents has the United States had? What special problems do minority presidents have?

★ Have any other elections in American history made changes in political alignments as decisive as those of 1860? What elections? Explain.

★ Buchanan and the Congress, between November 1860 and March 1861, were *lame ducks*. What does this mean? How did Amendment XX, ratified in 1933, reduce the length of the lame-duck period for president and Congress?

★ Soon after Lincoln's election, South Carolina seceded (December 20, 1860). According to the Constitution, what should or could President Buchanan have done when word of South Carolina's secession reached him? Would the Congress have supported strong action against South Carolina? Explain.

The Last Attempt at Compromise

It might have been possible to avoid disunion and civil war even after South Carolina's secession. The states of the Upper South—Virginia, Arkansas, Tennessee, and North Carolina—were not eager to secede. The Border states—Maryland, Delaware, Kentucky, and Missouri—wanted compromise. A last compromise was attempted. Senator John J. Crittenden of Kentucky proposed three amendments to the Constitution. (1) He proposed to restore the Missouri Compromise and extend its provisions to the Pacific coast. (2) He proposed to guarantee that the national government would never interfere with slavery inside a state. (3) He proposed to compensate slaveowners whose runaway slaves were rescued by Northerners who refused to return them. The *Crittenden Compromise* was tempting to those who feared civil war. Historians suggest that a large majority of the people were in favor of Crittenden's plan. The people, however, had no opportunity to vote on it.

The Crittenden Compromise was

The Presidential Election of 1860

	Popular Vote and Percentage		Electoral Vote and Percentage	
Abraham Lincoln (Rep.)	1,865,593	39.7%	180	59.4%
Stephen A. Douglas (N. Dem.)	1,382,713	29.5%	12	4.0%
John C. Breckinridge (S. Dem.)	848,356	18.1%	72	23.8%
John Bell (Const. Union)	592,306	12.7%	39	12.8%

How the states went:

17½ for Lincoln:	All the free states except half of New Jersey
11 for Breckinridge:	All the slave states except Missouri, Virginia, Kentucky, Tennessee
3 for Bell:	Virginia, Kentucky, Tennessee
1½ for Douglas:	Missouri and half of New Jersey

CHARLESTON

MERCURY

EXTRA:

Passed unanimously at 1.15 o'clock, P. M. December 20th, 1860.

AN ORDINANCE

To dissolve the Union between the State of South Carolina and other States united with her under the compact entitled " The Constitution of the United States of America."

We, the People of the State of South Carolina, in Convention assembled, do declare and ordain, and it is hereby declared and ordained,

That the Ordinance adopted by us in Convention, on the twenty-third day of May, in the year of our Lord one thousand seven hundred and eighty-eight, whereby the Constitution of the United States of America was ratified, and also, all Acts and parts of Acts of the General Assembly of this State, ratifying amendments of the said Constitution, are hereby repealed; and that the union now subsisting between South Carolina and other States, under the name of "The United States of America," is hereby dissolved.

THE

UNION

IS

DISSOLVED!

finally defeated in the Senate on January 16, 1861, by 25 to 23, with six Southern Democrats not voting. The crucial factor in the defeat of the compromise seems to have been the determination of Lincoln and the Republican leaders not to retreat from their platform promise *to prevent any further extension of slavery in the territories*. Abraham Lincoln was well aware of the terrible seriousness of the proposed amendment. Time and again, he wrote to fellow Republicans words like these:

Entertain no proposition in regard to the extension of slavery. The instant you do they have us under again: all our labor is lost, and sooner or later must be done over.[1]

Thus the last attempt at compromise failed, and a war that few Americans wanted loomed like a thundercloud.

● Should Lincoln have backed down for the sake of peace and union? What does his attitude at this crucial stage tell you about his character? What does it suggest about the grave responsibilities of a statesman at a time of crisis?

[1]Letter to William Kellogg, December 11, 1860, quoted in Allan Nevins, *The Emergence of Lincoln*, Volume II, *Prologue to Civil War* (New York: Charles Scribner's Sons, 1950), p. 394.

President Abraham Lincoln

2

The War for the Union— and the War for Southern Independence

War is the anger of bewildered peoples in front of questions they cannot answer.

War is the continuation of policy by other means.

These two quotations give two very different interpretations of war. The first is from a play, *Robert E. Lee,* by John Drinkwater. The second is from the Prussian student of war, General von Clausewitz.

● Explain in your own words the meaning of each quotation. Which of them sees war as a *rational* procedure? Can *both* quotations be correct? Think about these two points of view as you read about the American Civil War.

● Look at the title of this chapter. What does it suggest about the policy that each side set out to pursue "by other means"?

Why Did the Civil War Occur?

The two quotations at the head of the chapter remind us that the explanations of a war may be *at once irrational and rational.* Popular emotion, anger, and frustration may be a necessary condition. At the same time, there must be hard-headed political and military leaders who know what they want and what steps to take to get it.

Civil wars are often harder to explain than international wars. In an international war we can usually identify two or more nations or states whose leaders have certain policies. The policies may be conquest of territory, defense of national interests, domination of other nations, or preservation of the balance of power. In a civil war, however, the opposing sides usually take clear shape only after peace efforts break down. So do their policies. Moreover, individuals often choose sides *after* a civil war has started; they may choose for many differing reasons. Some may not want to take sides at all. Brothers may find themselves fighting on opposite sides; their parents may be uncertain which side they want to win.

The clashing economic interests of Northern industry with its free labor on one side and Southern cotton planters with their slave labor on the other helped push the states into the armed conflict of 1861. But historians disagree about the many other contributing causes of the Civil War. The *motives* of individual participants were even more complicated. Some men were fighting for slavery, some against it. Some were fighting for states' rights; some for preservation of the Union. Some were fighting for a way of life—for white supremacy or for democracy and human equality. Some were fighting for no clearly identifiable motive but merely because they had reached a pitch of fury and frustration after decades of sectional squabbling. Many fought merely because they were drafted.

● Beyond the mixed motives of individuals and groups often lie the motives of their leaders, which we may identify as their basic policies. Read carefully the following statements by Southern and Northern leaders. What basic policies can you identify?

1. Alexander Stephens, vice-president of the Confederacy, from a speech at Savannah, February 1861.

Our new government is founded upon exactly the opposite idea [from the idea of the equality of races]; its foundations are laid, its cornerstone rests upon the great truth, that the Negro is not equal to the white man; that slavery—subordination to the superior race—is his natural and normal condition.[1]

2. Jefferson Davis, president of the Confederacy, from his message to the Confederate Congress, April 29, 1861, just two weeks after Lincoln's call for troops to put down the rebellion.

Finally a great party was organized [in the North] for the purpose of obtaining the administration of the [national] Government, with the avowed object of using its power for the total exclusion of the slave States from all participation in the benefits of the public domain [U. S. territories] acquired by all the States in common . . . ; of surrounding them entirely by States in which slavery should be prohibited; of thus rendering the property in slaves so insecure as to be comparatively worthless, and thereby annihilating in effect property worth thousands of millions of dollars. This party, thus organized, succeeded in the month of November last in the election of its candidate for the Presidency of the United States.

. . . With interests of such overwhelming magnitude imperilled, the people of the Southern States were driven by the conduct of the North to the adoption of some course of action to avert the danger with which they were openly menaced. . . .

. . . the people of the Confederate States, in their conventions, determined that the wrongs which they had suffered and the evils with which they were menaced required that they should revoke the delegation of powers to the Federal Government which they had ratified in their several conventions [in 1788–89]. They consequently passed ordinances resuming all their rights as sovereign and independent States and dissolved their connection with the other States of the Union.[2]

3. From the Mississippi convention's statement on secession, January 26, 1861.

Utter subjugation awaits us in the Union, if we should consent longer to remain in it. It is not a matter of choice, but of necessity. We must either submit to degradation and to loss of property worth four billions of money, or we must secede from the Union framed by our fathers, to secure this as well as every other species of property. For far less cause than this our fathers separated from the Crown of England.[3]

---

[1]This speech, as well as many of the other quotations, may be found in many collections of historical documents. See, e.g., Hugh T. Lefler (ed.), *A History of the United States from the Age of Exploration to 1865* (New York: Meridian, 1960), p. 368.

[2]The version of Jefferson Davis's speech is from Robert Birley (ed.), *Speeches and Documents in American History*, Vol. II, 1818–1865. (London: Oxford University Press, 1944), pp. 264–66.

[3]Hugh T. Lefler, *op. cit.*, p. 367.

General Robert E. Lee

4. Lincoln's first Inaugural Address, March 4, 1861, began by specifically denying any intention of interfering with slavery in the states, promising to protect slave property, agreeing that fugitive slaves should be returned. Lincoln went on to denounce any attempt to break up the federal Union as illegal.

It follows from these views that no State upon its own mere motion can lawfully get out of the Union; that resolves and ordinances to that effect are legally void; and that acts of violence, within any State or States, against the authority of the United States are insurrectionary or revolutionary, according to circumstances.

I therefore consider that . . . the Union is unbroken; and to the extent of my ability I shall take care, as the Constitution itself expressly enjoins upon me, that the laws of the Union be faithfully executed in all the States.

Lincoln went on to appeal for unity and mutual confidence and to praise the idea of government by the people and majority rule. He equated secession with anarchy. Speaking to the South, he added:

In your hands, my dissatisfied fellow-countrymen, and not in mine, is the momentous issue of civil war. The [national] government will not assail you. You can have no conflict without being yourselves the aggressors. You have no oath registered in heaven to destroy the government, while I shall have the most solemn one to 'preserve, protect, and defend' it.[4]

5. From Lincoln's proclamation of April 15, 1861, after the fall of Fort Sumter.

Whereas the laws of the United States have been for some time past and now are opposed, and the execution thereof obstructed, in the States of South Carolina, Georgia, Alabama, Florida, Mississippi, Louisiana, and Texas by combinations too powerful to be suppressed by the ordinary course of judicial proceedings or by the powers vested in the marshals by law:

Now, therefore, I, Abraham Lincoln, President of the United States, in virtue of the power in me vested by the Constitution and the laws, have thought fit to call forth, and hereby do call forth, the militia of the several States of the Union to the aggregate numbers of 75,000, in order to suppress said combinations and to cause the laws to be duly executed.[5]

6. A year and a half later, Lincoln expressed his objective in the war, in a famous letter to Horace Greeley, editor of the *New York Tribune*. Greeley had attacked Lincoln for not emancipating the slaves. Lincoln's open reply included the following statement.

As to the policy I "seem to be pursuing," as you say, I have not meant to leave any one in doubt.

I would save the Union. I would save it the shortest way under the Con-

stitution. The sooner the national authority can be restored, the nearer the Union will be "the Union as it was." If there be those who would not save the Union unless they could at the same time *save* Slavery, I do not agree with them. If there be those who would not save the Union unless they could at the same time *destroy* Slavery, I do not agree with them. My paramount object in this struggle *is* to save the Union, and is *not* either to save or destroy Slavery. If I could save the Union without freeing *any* slave, I would do it; and if I could save it by freeing *all* the slaves, I would do it; and if I could do it by freeing some and leaving others alone, I would also do that. What I do about Slavery and the colored race, I do because I believe it helps to save this Union; and what I forbear, I forbear because I do *not* believe it would help to save the Union. . . . I have here stated my purpose according to my view of *official* duty, and I intend no modification of my oft-expressed *personal* wish that all men, everywhere could be free.[6]

The First Act of War

The two sides and their policies took shape gradually in the six months following the election. The decisive event was the attack on Fort Sumter, April 12–13, 1861. This federal fortress stood in the harbor of Charleston, South Carolina. Under President Buchanan, a half-hearted attempt was made to send supplies to the handful of United States soldiers in Fort Sumter. The steamer turned back, however, when it was fired on by South Carolinian troops. A month after Lincoln's inauguration, a second attempt to send supplies was made. This time Confederate troops attacked the fort *before* the supply ship arrived. The federal troops, with hardly any food or ammunition and with

---

[4]See Robert Birley, *op. cit.*, pp. 240–50.

[5]See Hugh T. Lefler, *op. cit.*, p. 371.

[6]Robert Birley, *op. cit.*, pp. 276–77.

The attack on Fort Sumter

the fortress on fire, had to surrender. The Southern attack on Fort Sumter was of immense psychological value to Lincoln. Many Northerners, indignant over the attack, supported Lincoln when he responded by calling out the militia and ordering an emergency session of Congress.

The effect of Lincoln's calling for 75,000 troops was less helpful in the South. Only then (April 17–May 20) did Virginia, Arkansas, Tennessee, and North Carolina join the Confederate States. There was still a possibility that the Border states of Maryland, Delaware, Kentucky, and Missouri might swing to the Southern cause. However, these states did not secede. The disturbing dilemma faced by many Americans was summed up in Robert E. Lee's poignant letter of April 20, 1861, to his sister, who supported Lincoln.

With all my devotion to the Union and the feeling of loyalty and duty of an American citizen, I have not been able to make up my mind to raise my hand against my relatives, my children, my home. I have therefore resigned my commission in the Army, and save in defense of my native State, with the sincere hope that my poor services may never be needed, I hope I may never be called on to draw my sword.[7]

- The decision to send supplies to Fort Sumter was Lincoln's personal decision. General Winfield Scott and five out of seven members of Lincoln's cabinet opposed the decision. What do *you* think of Lincoln's decision?

- Would you say that the Confederate leaders made a serious mistake in attacking Fort Sumter? Explain.

- Lincoln's decision to call up 75,000 troops without congressional approval has been described as unconstitutional. Do you agree? Explain.

[7]Robert Birley, *op. cit.*, p. 259.

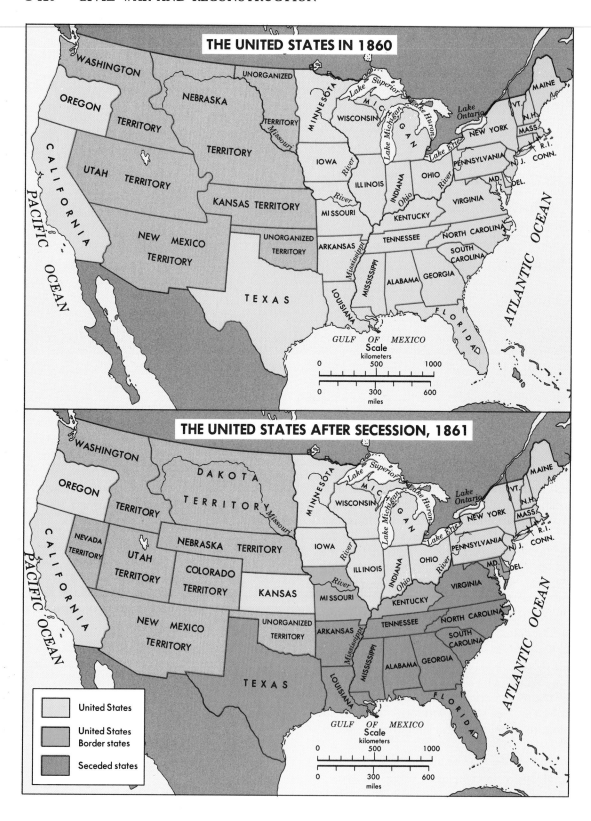

Jefferson Davis

Alexander Stephens

Strategies

Military experts make a distinction between strategy and tactics. *Strategy* is the overall plan for gaining one's policy objective. *Tactics* is the procedure on the battlefield.

In the Civil War each side developed a strategy to suit its objective. The objective of the North was to reunify the nation; that of the South was to achieve independence.

► Which side would need to *conquer* the other to attain its objective?

● What was the objective of the British and that of the Patriots in the American Revolutionary War? Are they comparable to the objectives of the North and the South in the Civil War? Explain.

★ What is the difference between a *limited* war and a *total* (all-out) war? In which class would you place the American Civil War? Was it a *limited war for one side* and a *total war for the other?* Explain.

In deciding on a strategic plan, political and military leaders have to consider many things in addition to their objectives. They must take account of their own *resources* and those of the enemy. They must think about *military technology* and *tactics. Geography* is of central importance. The *time factor,* too, must be considered: Is an early decisive victory necessary? Or is it to your advantage to let the war drag out? A leader must also ask himself *whether other powers will intervene* in the war and, if so, on which side. Finally, *psychological* factors are important. Is public opinion favorable to carrying on the war? Or is it weak and weary? Is the *morale* of troops and people high or low?

Some Resources of North and South, 1861

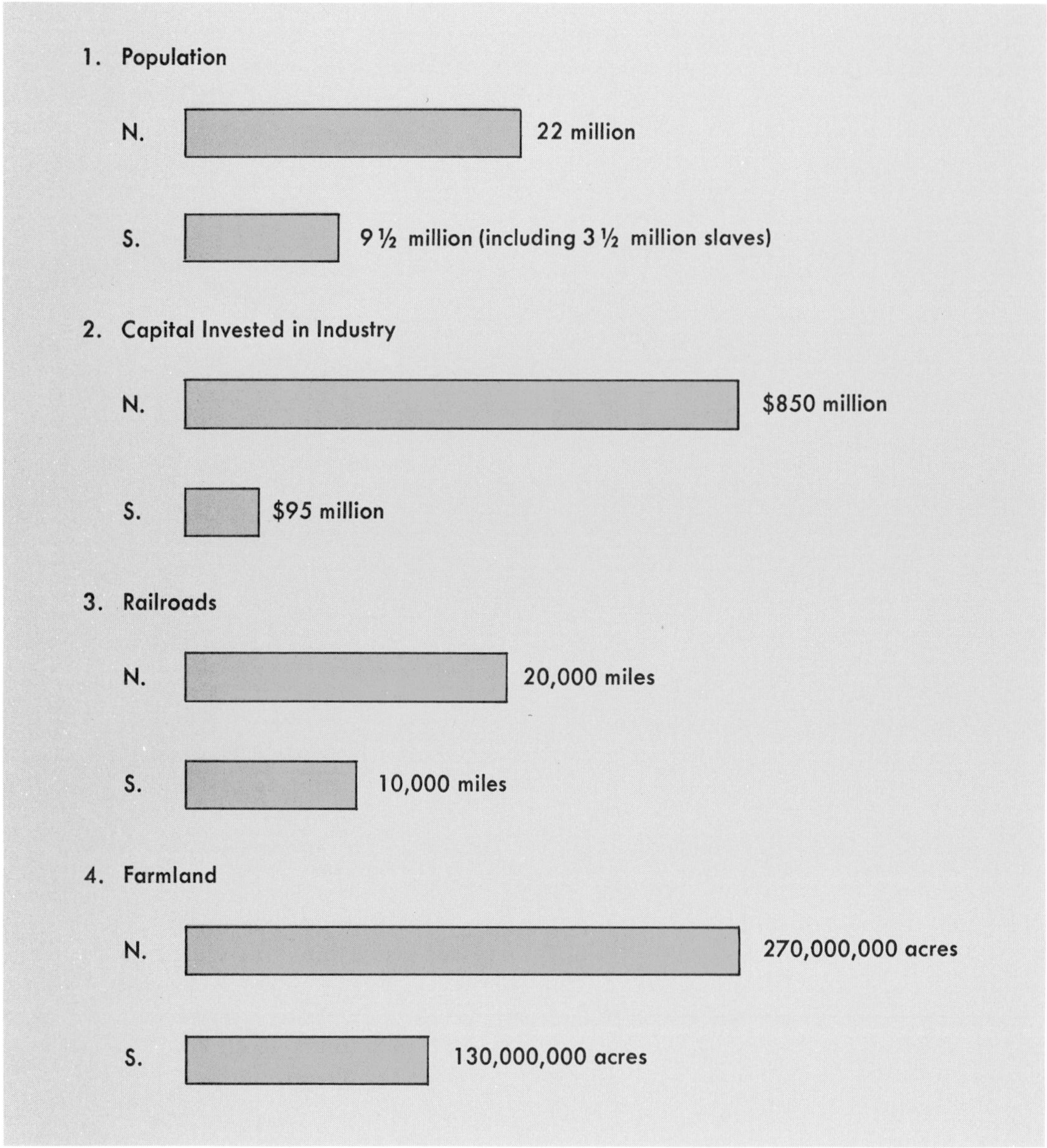

1. Population

N. [bar] 22 million

S. [bar] 9 ½ million (including 3 ½ million slaves)

2. Capital Invested in Industry

N. [bar] $850 million

S. [bar] $95 million

3. Railroads

N. [bar] 20,000 miles

S. [bar] 10,000 miles

4. Farmland

N. [bar] 270,000,000 acres

S. [bar] 130,000,000 acres

● Look at the bar graphs on this page showing comparative resources of the North and South. Do you think the South had a good chance of gaining its objective? Why or why not? (Many people of the North and of the South, and most astute European observers, thought that the South surely would win independence for itself.)

● In population the North was much larger than the South. The North had 22 million people. The South had nearly 9 million, of whom 3,600,000 were blacks, most of them slaves. In the North and the Border states there were 800,000 black people. At first, Northern blacks were not allowed to serve in the armed forces, but later on about 200,000 were soldiers or sailors. How would these population facts affect the chances of victory? How would slaves help the South?

★ How did the population and wealth of Britain and of the 13 colonies compare in 1776? How might these figures affect Southern hopes in 1861?

New Technology and the War

In the field of military technology, the American Civil War was a turning point in history. The war was the first war fought with the new technology of industrial societies. That new technology included railroads, steamships, ironclad warships, *rifled* artillery, and, above all, *rifled* muskets. *Breechloading rifles* and *carbines* also were used. Not surprisingly, the leaders and generals on both sides were slow to recognize how these new factors affected both strategy and tactics. Lack of adjustment to the new technology was responsible for the fearful slaughter in many of the battles of the war. Often 50 per cent of the infantry soldiers in an attack were killed or wounded; sometimes the proportion rose to 80 or even 90 per cent. Now, every soldier wears a "dog tag" so that his body can be identified. In the Civil War there were no dog tags, but soldiers knew how likely they were to be killed. Before an attack they would print their names and next-of-kin on handkerchiefs which they stitched on the backs of their uniforms.

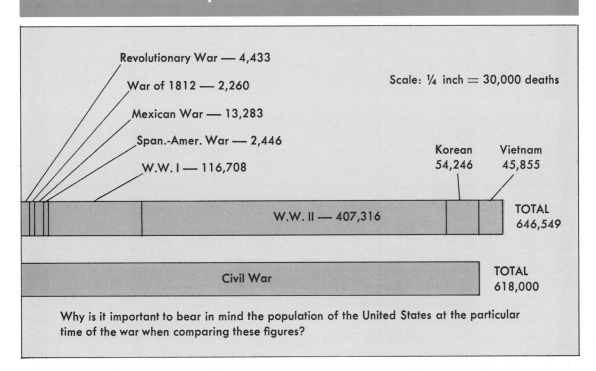

Civil War Deaths as Compared with United States Casualties in Other Wars

Revolutionary War — 4,433
War of 1812 — 2,260
Mexican War — 13,283
Span.-Amer. War — 2,446
W.W. I — 116,708

Scale: ¼ inch = 30,000 deaths

Korean 54,246   Vietnam 45,855

W.W. II — 407,316

TOTAL 646,549

Civil War

TOTAL 618,000

Why is it important to bear in mind the population of the United States at the particular time of the war when comparing these figures?

Smooth-Bore Muskets and Rifled Muskets

The Old Smooth-Bore Musket

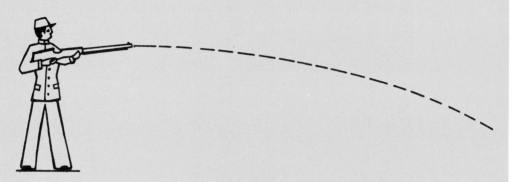

Killing range about 50 yards: "Don't fire until you see the whites of their eyes!"
Could be loaded only standing or kneeling because powder, wadding, and bullet
had to be dropped down the barrel and rammed firm. A man could fire one shot
every two or three minutes.

The Muzzle-Loading, Percussion-Cap, Rifled Musket

Killing range about 500 yards. Could be loaded only standing or kneeling. One or
more shots could be fired each minute. (Breechloading rifles also came into use.
These could be loaded while the soldier was lying prone. Carbines, which could fire
several shots a minute, had also been invented, but were not much used: the problem
of supplying ammunition was too great. Some machine guns were also used.)

● When the Civil War began, the usual method of attack was that which had been used since the seventeenth century. Infantry with muskets and bayonets would march and charge in close order against the enemy. The enemy might fire one or two volleys before the two lines of defenders and attackers fought hand-to-hand. Sometimes heavy cavalry would charge the defending lines. Generals during the Civil War tried to continue these tactics, but the attackers suffered terrible losses, while the defenders were often surprised at their own relatively small losses. Why did the attackers begin to suffer the heavier losses? Look at the diagram on page C-132 for some clues. What new tactics or new technology might be needed when defensive weapons were so devastating?

● It has been said that the leaders of neither side "guessed at the power and ferocity with which the other would arise to the struggle. Both were to emerge in the end to confront a toll of death and suffering, devastation and bitterness so disproportionate to the original issues that even today there is little agreement as to just what the 'causes' were or how they engendered a catastrophe of such appalling magnitude."[8]

[8]Walter Millis, *Arms and Men: A Study of American Military History* (New York: Mentor, 1958), p. 102.

Could the leaders be excused on the grounds that the war was technologically unprecedented? Explain.

The railroads, like the rifle, made a great difference to war. In the past, armies were necessarily fairly small, because of supply problems. In the Mexican War, for example, the total number under arms during the whole war was about 100,000 men.[9] The railway, however, made it possible not only to move tens of thousands of men rapidly, but also to keep a hundred thousand or more supplied with food and ammunition. During the Civil War, about two million men fought or served in the Union armies. Of course, reliance on the railroad also *limited the area* in which large forces could operate. It took time to lay new tracks.

[9]*Ibid.*, p. 93.

The second Battle of Bull Run, August 30, 1862

Even with the aid of the telegraph, it was extremely difficult for generals to control the huge forces that fought the later battles of the Civil War. A whole new staff system had to be worked out. Better maps were needed. As it was, ordinary soldiers and field officers often had no idea where they were or what they were doing. One general, when ordered to attack, said he was all set to do so, if only he could be told in which direction the enemy lay! Battles were lost because whole divisions marched the wrong way or ended up ten miles or more from the place they were supposed to be.

Thus, the American Civil War was a new kind of war. The blood of hundreds of thousands of young men was shed while military leaders were trying to learn a new type of warfare—the warfare of mass armies based on industrial societies.

● It has been said that in industrialized mass warfare winning a battle is hardly ever decisive. What counts is the long, slow process in which superior resources and manpower finally wear the weaker side down. Does this generalization seem to apply to the Civil War?

★ Has the generalization been true of all the great wars in the late nineteenth and the twentieth century? What exceptions are there? (World War II looked as if it would be an exception in 1940.)

Geography and Strategy

The geography that military planners must consider includes a number of factors. *Physical features* are important since they constitute barriers to or routes for military movement. *Cultural features* are equally important. Highways, railroads, bridges, key cities, ports, and industrial and agricultural areas must be carefully weighed in terms of their value to one's own side and to the enemy.

● Look at the map on page C-135. Which major physical features seem of special importance militarily? Why?

● Which section had the better railroad network? At what points was the South's railroad system most vulnerable?

● Do you think the ports of the Confederacy were important in the war effort? Why?

● Find out capitals of the Union and the Confederacy. How far apart were they? How might their closeness affect strategic plans?

● What strategy would you choose (a) if you were Lincoln and his generals? (b) If you were Davis and his generals?

The main military efforts in the first year of the war were almost entirely in Virginia. General Lee and General Jackson threatened Washington; General McClellan threatened Richmond. Then, as time went on, the Union leaders, especially Grant and Sherman, saw the importance of the western areas of the Confederacy. They struck south into Tennessee and down the Mississippi to Vicksburg. Admiral Farragut took New Orleans from the sea. Thus the Union controlled the Mississippi River by mid-1863: Texas, Louisiana, and Arkansas were cut off from the rest of the Confederacy.

Meanwhile, Lee invaded Maryland and Pennsylvania, but suffered such cruel losses at Antietam (September 1862) and Gettysburg (July 1863) that he was forced to retreat into Virginia.

The Southern city of Vicksburg fell on July 4, 1863, and the battle of Gettysburg came to an end on the same day. The Southern losses were, probably, the real turning point of the war. Thereafter the Union troops advanced deep into the Confederacy from the west (Chickamauga, Chattanooga, Atlanta, and Savannah) and then northward through the Carolinas.

This was Sherman's famous campaign, which left a trail of destruction. At the same time Grant advanced slowly, bloody battle following bloody battle, through Virginia.

● Look at the map on page C-135. Why did the loss of Chattanooga and Atlanta practically seal the fate of the Confederacy?

● One important part of Union strategy was the *blockading* of Southern ports. Why?

● What was Lee's object in invading Maryland and Pennsylvania? Did he hope to conquer territory in the North? Explain.

The Time Factor and the South's Hope of Foreign Intervention

For the Union, an early decisive victory was especially desirable. It might have been achieved in 1862, when General McClellan planned to take Richmond and defeat Lee's army in a *combined operation*

THE MAIN RAILROADS IN OPERATION IN 1860

Boundary of Confederacy
Railroads

(that is, with units of the army and the navy in cooperation). The plan failed, possibly because Lincoln interfered, possibly because McClellan was too indecisive.

● Considering the final outcome of the war, do you consider McClellan's failure to achieve a decisive victory in 1862 a great tragedy? Explain.

★ Find out more about McClellan's peninsula campaign and the Seven Day's Battle, June 26–July 2, 1862.

For the Confederacy an early decisive victory was almost out of the question, so Jefferson Davis and other Southern leaders decided to rely upon a prolonged conflict and hope that time would bring two possible developments. First, popular feeling in the North might turn against the war. People weary of fighting might end the war, even at the cost of letting the South become independent. The South's second hope was that European powers, especially Britain and France, would recognize the Confederacy. Those powers might help with money, naval support, and—just possibly—armed force. Davis's advisers told him that Britain needed Southern cotton so badly that it would not permit the North to blockade Southern ports. Moreover, Britain had been sympathetic to movements of national independence in Greece, Latin America, and Italy. Surely it would sympathize with the Confederacy!

★ What precedent in American history might encourage Jefferson Davis's hopes of foreign intervention?

★ Many influential British leaders favored the Southern cause. What strong section of British public opinion favored the North? Why? What moral issue influenced British opinion?

★ An early episode that might have brought Britain into the war was the

Trent affair. What was that about?

Whether the British government would have recognized the South in spite of opposition at home is an open question. But such recognition was possible only if the South could prevent the North from achieving important victories. Unfortunately for Jefferson Davis, time ran out. Late in 1862 and in 1863 came the Southern losses at Antietam, Vicksburg, and Gettysburg. The British government, which had been considering recognizing the South, decided not to do so.

★ How did the British defeat at Saratoga, in 1777, affect foreign intervention in the American Revolution?

The Psychological Factor in the North

Napoleon once said: "In war, the *moral* [psychological] is to the *physical* as three to one." He meant that troops whose spirit and courage are high may defeat three times their number of low-spirited troops. With the coming of mass industrial wars, not merely the fighting troops but the civilians need a high spirit and determination if they are to support the war.

One of Lincoln's serious problems was division and uncertainty in the North. He himself was far from popular with many groups in 1860. After the war broke out and the Union suffered a number of humiliating defeats, much more opposition arose in the North. Editors and cartoonists portrayed the chief executive as a moron or a tyrant responsible for the country's setbacks. "Peace Democrats" wondered how many thousands of men would have to be slaughtered before the Lincoln administration entered into negotiations with the Confederacy to end the war. Although they said they wished to restore the Union, this faction demanded an end to all fighting. They proposed a national convention to amend the Constitution so as to guarantee states' rights. Many of these "Peace Democrats" were of the opinion that Lincoln's stubbornness alone was responsible for prolonging the conflict. Within this faction was a group called the "Copperheads." Some of them favored peace at any cost and spoke in favor of creating a Western Confederacy to further divide the United States. A number of secret Copperhead societies were formed. People claimed that these societies engaged in treasonable activities to assist the Confederacy.

★ How did Lincoln deal with the opponents to the Civil War? Was his suspension of the *writ of habeas corpus* constitutional? Was it justifiable?

★ Investigate the Supreme Court decisions involving *ex parte Merryman* and *ex parte Milligan*. How did these attempts help to restore the civil rights which had been violated? Were they effective?

★ The foremost leader of the Copperheads was Clement L. Vallandigham of Ohio. What became of him?

★ What parallels and what differences can you see between "Mr. Lincoln's War," and "Mr. Madison's War," and "Mr. Johnson's War"? Explain.

★ Although Lincoln had troubles with his cabinet, partially because of the incompetence of some cabinet members, at least three members were outstanding: William Seward, Salmon P. Chase, and Edward Stanton. Find out more about these men.

Lincoln and his Cabinet. (Seated left to right) Stanton, Secretary of War; Lincoln; Welles, Secretary of the Navy; Seward, Secretary of State; Bates, Attorney General. (Standing) Chase, Secretary of the Treasury; Smith, Secretary of the Interior; and Blair, Postmaster General

The Psychological Factor in the South

Jefferson Davis, at first, was more fortunate than Lincoln in the matter of popular support, for the Southern people seemed from the outset more united and sure of themselves and their aim — independence and protection of their way of life — than were the people of the North. Even so, Davis ran into considerable difficulty in gaining effective cooperation. This difficulty stemmed from the very nature of the Confederacy. The states of the South, instead of viewing themselves as parts of a nation, insisted that each was sovereign. They wanted the Confederacy to win its independence. Yet during the war, their stubborn and blind devotion to states' rights actually contributed to their own defeat. At some crucial periods, several governors refused to cooperate with Davis. In 1864, for instance, the governor of Georgia refused to permit the state militia to help defend Richmond, the capital of the Confederacy. He said they must remain in their native state as its "only remaining protection against the encroachment of centralized power"!

Then there was the problem of the president's cabinet. Davis at first selected the members almost entirely on a geographical basis. He wanted to include a representative from each state except his own Mississippi. The result was an unstable group. By the time the war ended, there had been three secretaries of state, two secretaries of the treasury, four attorneys general, and five secretaries of war. Few were really competent. Perhaps that was why Davis did not pay much attention to their advice.

Finally, there was the problem of the vice-president, Alexander Stephens of Georgia. Actually Stephens opposed secession for three months after Lincoln's election, and he accepted the vice-presidency of the Confederacy with reluctance. He was convinced that the rights of the states were being infringed upon even by the new government of the South. For this reason, he repeatedly and openly charged that Davis was a tyrant who should be impeached. Instead of assisting Davis, Stephens became the leader of the political opposition. As vice-president, he was president of the Senate, and in this position he assisted in the passage of many laws which conflicted with Davis's policies. Davis vetoed 39 measures by the Confederate Congress, whereas Lincoln used the veto power on only three occasions.

- ● The Confederacy had no political parties as such. Would they have developed had the Confederacy survived? Explain.

- ★ Look at the *Constitution of the Confederate States of America*. In what important ways did it differ from that of the United States of America? See especially the Preamble; Article I, Sections 6 (2); 8 (1) and (3); 9 (1), (2), (4), (6), and (9); Article IV, Sections 2 and 3.

- ★ Investigate the biographies of Alexander Stephens, Davis's outspoken opponent, and of Judah P. Benjamin, the Jewish man from Louisiana who was probably Davis's most competent cabinet member. How did these two Confederates differ in political philosophy?

War Is Hell

The Northern general William Tecumseh Sherman once remarked: "War is hell." This was made clear to the people of Georgia and the Carolinas as his army marched through these states, looting and burning to destroy the people's will to resist.

The American Civil War was perhaps unusually infernal. Not only was it a civil war, with all the special bitterness that civil wars have, but it was also a war fought with a new and devastating technology that few, if any, of the participants had ever foreseen. Everyone completely miscalculated the extent of the suffering and damage that would result. An early victory for the North or an early compromise peace might have prevented much of the agony. Perhaps neither of these possibilities was out of the question in 1862, but the very fact of divisions and internal squabbles on both sides probably made the leaders more nervous. The leaders were, therefore, less capable either of quick deci-

sive action or of offering a compromise, since the latter would have seemed a sign of weakness.

Once the war was over, people tended to forget these confusions and uncertainties. When a clear pattern did finally emerge, and a clear victory was attained, Lincoln had indeed become a heroic leader who "belongs to the ages." But the student of history must not ignore the troubled anguish of the years of decision. "War is the anger of bewildered people . . ." as well as "the continuation of policy by other means."

Jefferson Davis and his Cabinet (seated left to right) Judah P. Benjamin, attorney-general; Stephen M. Mallory, Secretary of the Navy; Alexander H. Stephens, Vice-President; Jefferson Davis, President; John H. Regan, Postmaster-General; Robert Toombs, Secretary of State; (standing left to right) Charles G. Memminger, Secretary of the Treasury; and, Leroy P. Walker, Secretary of War.

The Battle of Antietem, September 17, 1862

The Battle of Gettysburg, June 27–July 4, 1863

3
Battles and Events of the War

The War Takes Shape

In 1861 and 1862, the leaders of both sides were fumbling for strategies and organization. Lincoln managed to keep the border slave states—Maryland, Delaware, Kentucky, and Missouri—in the Union. The western section of Virginia seceded from its parent state and joined the Union as the state of West Virginia.

North and South proceeded to build up their armies, and in July 1861 half-trained troops met in a battle at Manassas Junction in Virginia. This, the First Battle of Bull Run, ended in a rout of the Union troops. Washington was threatened, and Lincoln became aware of how open the capital was to Southern attack.

The Union navy was expanded, and the Confederacy was blockaded. This blockade was fairly ineffective until 1863–64, and many Southern ships were able to trade with Europe. In April 1862, Union ships and troops took New Orleans.

Meanwhile Union forces invaded Tennessee in the western theater, while indecisive battles took place in Virginia. However, in September 1862, a major battle took place in Maryland. Lee had invaded Maryland to threaten Washington and to cut its railroad communications with the North. McClellan's Army of the Potomac met Lee's Army of Northern Virginia at Antietam, where about 25 per cent of Lee's men were killed and wounded, as compared with about 15 per cent of McClellan's. McClellan did not push to a decisive victory, but Lee had to retreat to Virginia. The importance of Antietam was twofold: first, it discouraged Britain and France from recognizing the Confederacy; second, it encouraged Lincoln to take a stand on slavery.

The Emancipation Proclamation, January 1, 1863

For various reasons, Lincoln hesitated to make slavery as such an issue in the war.

● Why would Lincoln want to avoid the issue of slavery in the early months of the war?

Earlier in his career, Lincoln was a *colonizationist*. That is, he thought the solution to the race problem was to send freed slaves to Africa or Haiti. In the first year of his presidency, he sided with Northern Democrats and conservative Republicans in Congress. Several times he proposed gradual emancipation, compensation to owners, and transportation of free blacks overseas. These proposals were un-

Immediately after emancipation was proclaimed, freed black people came into the Union Lines at New Bern, North Carolina

successful. In July 1861, Congress voted the *Crittenden Resolution.* The resolution stated that the aim of the Union was *not* to interfere with slavery in any state.

The more radical Republicans continued to demand immediate freeing of all slaves. Lincoln gradually moved in this direction. In April 1862, Congress freed the slaves in the District of Columbia and paid their owners up to $300 for each freed black. In June of the same year, Congress abolished slavery in all territories. In July, Lincoln announced that all fugitive slaves from the South would be free. In the same month, he showed a draft emancipation proclamation to his cabinet. Most members of the cabinet were against the proposal.

Lincoln, however, waited for a good moment to act. Antietam gave him that moment. Five days after the victory, he issued the *Preliminary Emancipation Proclamation.* It stated that on January 1, 1863, all slaves in states still in rebellion would

be free. The Confederate States had 100 days to rejoin the Union. In the North, the preliminary proclamation was far from popular. However, on the first day of 1863, Lincoln published the *Emancipation Proclamation:*

I do order and declare that all persons held as slaves within said designated States [the Confederacy] are, and henceforward shall be free. . . .

And I further declare . . . that such persons of suitable condition, will be received into the armed service of the United States to garrison forts, positions, stations, and other places, and to man vessels of all sorts in said service.

► How many slaves gained their freedom on January 1, 1863?

● Lincoln used to be praised as "the Great Emancipator." Later, critics said the emancipation was only a political maneuver. What do you think?

● How did the Emancipation Proclamation help the United States *diplomatically* in Europe?

● How does the account of Lincoln's progress toward the proclamation illustrate the division of opinion in the North on the war?

The Emancipation Proclamation marked an important change in the Union government's attitude toward black soldiers and sailors. Ever since the war started, Afro Americans had been trying to enlist, but many whites for various reasons were opposed to Negroes in the army and navy.

★ An example of white racial prejudice was the *draft riots* in New York, July 1863. Find out about these riots. An historian suggests that there was a connection between Northern white racial prejudice and the uncertainty of the national government's policies.[1] What do you think?

From spring 1863, more and more blacks joined the armed forces. About 93,000 came from the seceded states, 40,000 from the Border states, and 52,000 from the free states. Of these, 38,000 gave their lives. For over a year black servicemen were paid only half as much as white soldiers and sailors, but in 1864 they gained the right to equal pay. Negroes, when captured by Confederate forces, were treated much worse than white prisoners. Sometimes they were shot out of hand. About 200,000 blacks also worked for the army and navy as civilian laborers.

[1] John Hope Franklin, *From Slavery to Freedom: A History of Negro Americans* (New York: Knopf, 1969), p. 279.

Tenniel, the cartoonist, saw the Emancipation Proclamation as nothing more than a gesture by a wily gambler

In New York City, volunteers were sought by offering bounties to enlist or re-enlist

● Why were the Confederate forces especially cruel to black prisoners?

★ How did the Confederacy use slaves in its war effort? Think of construction work. Think of slave labor freeing white farmers for service in the army.

★ What part did Frederick Douglass play in recruiting black soldiers and sailors?

Some historians have noted that in the South slavery tended to create a division between the wealthy slaveowner and the poor white. Many poor whites in the South failed to support the Civil War not because they were opposed to slavery; rather they felt it senseless to risk their lives in order to maintain a system beneficial only to the wealthy. This feeling of class distinction in the Confederacy was confirmed by such things as the law that exempted from military service one white man on each plantation with 20 or more slaves. Owing to its unpopularity, this measure was later repealed.

● In 1865, the Confederate Congress authorized the drafting of 300,000 slaves to fight for the Southern cause. Why was this incongruous?

● Why were there no major slave rebellions in the South during the war?

Armies and Leaders

The Union had little difficulty when it came to obtaining men and supplies. At first, the volunteer system, aided by generous cash bounties, induced more than enough enlistments. When these began to dwindle, however, Congress enacted the first *national draft law* in American history. This was used primarily as a threat to urge men to enlist voluntarily. By 1865, only 46,000 men had been actually drafted in the Union army, out of nearly two million who served. Many others volunteered but were rejected for various reasons. As for supplies, the federal government had both the wealth and the factories to keep the average soldier well equipped for battle.

In the area of leadership Lincoln experienced his greatest difficulties. The first Union commander was Winfield Scott who had served in the War of 1812 and was a hero of the Mexican War. Owing to his advanced age, this very competent general was retired in 1861. He was succeeded by George McClellan. Historians generally agree that McClellan was a competent administrator and trainer, yet he failed as a leader in battle. McClellan was a great strategist, but only on paper. Others who replaced him likewise fell short of what Lincoln wanted: a decisive general who could win decisive battles and win the war

After Frederick Douglass spoke to President Lincoln about how black soldiers were treated, recruiting posters like this were common in the North

quickly. Finally, Ulysses S. Grant proved to be the man for whom the president had been searching, and in 1864 he was appointed general in chief of the Union armies.

★ Investigate the bounty system during the Civil War. Is there a type of bounty system used today to induce men to enlist in the armed forces?

★ Find out the origin of the word *shoddy* as it is used in the phrase "shoddy aristocracy." When, where, and why did this social class emerge?

Jefferson Davis did not experience a problem in finding capable generals. Perhaps because of the strong military tradition in the South, there was an abundance of talent: Robert E. Lee, Thomas "Stonewall" Jackson, J. E. B. Stuart, G. T. Beauregard, Patrick R. Cleburne, Joseph E. Johnston, and Nathan Bedford Forrest among others. Robert E. Lee is considered by many to be America's greatest general.

On the other hand, in the matter of military supplies the agricultural South was sadly lacking. Without the factories to manufacture such necessities as weapons, clothing, and shoes, and without the means of importing them from Europe because of a lack of credit and the Union blockade, the Confederate soldier had to devote a great deal of time to foraging for whatever he could find to stave off hunger and cold. As the chances for a Southern victory grew dimmer, enthusiasm for the war declined sharply, and enlistments dropped. The Confederate Congress attempted to deal with this manpower shortage by enacting several *conscription acts*. These provided relatively few men, however. In addition, Davis was thwarted by several governors who defended states' rights and who contended that conscription was illegal and certified a large

General Ulysses S. Grant

number of exemptions on their own authority. Add to this the large number of desertions (there were at least 100,000) and one can understand why there were probably fewer than 100,000 men in the Confederate Army, by the conclusion of the war.

- ★ What social and historical factors contributed to the South's military tradition?

- ★ Study a biography of Robert E. Lee or of Ulysses S. Grant. Why do some historians maintain that Lee was America's greatest general, even though the South lost the Civil War?

- ★ Jefferson Davis was a graduate of West Point. How did this contribute to friction between him and most of his generals?

The Battles of the War

The study of the battles of the Civil War is fascinating, but too complex for the present volume. The charts on pages C-147–C-148 provide a summary of important facts about the battles. Notice that they are classified under three headings—Eastern Campaign, 1861–63; Western Campaign, 1862–63; Closing Campaigns, 1864–65. It was not until the middle of 1863 that the net of the Union armies began to close in on the capital of the Confederacy.

It is probably true that certain battles, early in the war, were decisive in the sense that the failure of the South to win clear victories turned the tide in favor of the North. The Southern failure to defeat or "bottle-up" McClellan in the *Seven Days' Battle* in the summer of 1862 was grave. The losses and retreats at *Antietam* and *Gettysburg* encouraged the North and discouraged foreign intervention. The fall of *Vicksburg* in July 1863 split the Confederacy in two. The decisive Northern victory at *Chattanooga* late in 1863 severely hampered the Confederacy by cutting its main east-west railway link. Thereafter the heavy advantage of the North in men and material worked to grind the Southern armies to helplessness and surrender.

Two Crucial Battles: Vicksburg and Gettysburg

Let us look briefly at the two great Union victories of summer 1863.

By mid-1862 the North controlled New Orleans, at the mouth of the Mississippi, and the river north of Vicksburg. But Vicksburg itself held out. It was a city on high bluffs on the left bank, surrounded by a network of defenses. Confederate artillery commanded the waters of the Mississippi. Could the North seize this vital control point?

Admiral Farragut moved his gunboats from New Orleans toward Vicksburg in May 1862, but realized that a naval attack would be hopeless. The gunboats continued to patrol the river south of Vicksburg.

Major Battles of the Civil War

Eastern Battles 1861-1863	Date	Commanders		Result
		Union	Confederate	
First Bull Run *(Manassas)	July 21, 1861	McDowell	Beauregard	Confederate victory sobered the North.
Fair Oaks (Seven Pines)	May 31-June 1, 1862	McClellan	Johnston	Rebels driven back toward Richmond.
Seven Days	June 25-July 1, 1862	McClellan	Lee	Richmond saved; North retreated.
Second Bull Run	August 29-30, 1862	Pope	Lee	South commanded almost all Virginia.
Antietam (Sharpsburg)	September 17, 1862	McClellan	Lee	Union victory. (Technical)
Fredericksburg	December 13, 1862	Burnside	Lee	North defeated badly.
Chancellorsville	May 1-4, 1863	Hooker	Lee	Confederate victory.
Gettysburg	July 1-3, 1863	Meade	Lee	Union victory marked turning point in war.

*Names in parentheses refer to Southern names for battles.

Western Battles 1862-1863	Date	Commanders		Result
		Union	Confederate	
Fort Henry	February 6, 1862	Grant	Tilghman	Began Grant's western campaign.
Fort Donelson	February 16, 1862	Grant	Buckner	Northern victory.
Shiloh (Pittsburgh Landing)	April 6-7, 1862	Grant	Johnston, Beauregard	Grant taken by surprise, but still Union victory.
Perryville	October 8, 1862	Buell	Bragg	Confederate troops driven out of Kentucky.
Murfreesboro (Stones River)	December 31, 1862-January 2, 1863	Rosecrans	Bragg	Confederate victory; not followed up.
Vicksburg [siege]	May 19-July 4, 1863	Grant	Pemberton	Decisive Northern victory.
Chickamauga	September 19-20, 1863	Rosecrans	Bragg	Southern victory.
Chattanooga	November 23-25, 1863	Grant	Bragg	Union victory.

Major Battles of the War: Closing Campaigns, 1864-65

Battle	Date	Commanders		Result
		Union	Confederate	
The Wilderness	May 5-6, 1864	Grant	Lee	Union victory but heavy losses.
Spotsylvania Court House	May 8-12, 1864	Grant	Lee	Drawn battle.
Cold Harbor	June 3, 1864	Grant	Lee	Heavy Northern losses.
Petersburg [siege]	June 20, 1864- April 2, 1865	Grant	Lee	Nine-month siege weakened Lee's forces.
Kennesaw Mountain	June 27, 1864	Sherman	Johnston	Confederate success.
Mobile Bay	August 5, 1864	Farragut	Buchanan	Mobile blockaded.
Sherman's March	November 15- December 22, 1864	Sherman	Johnston	Sherman conquered Georgia almost unopposed, occupied Savannah. Battles for Atlanta of major importance to North.
Nashville	December 15-16, 1864	Thomas	Hood	Northern victory ended resistance in West.
Invasion of the Carolinas	January 16- March 21, 1865	Sherman	Johnston	Sherman occupied both Carolinas.

The burden then fell on the shoulders of General Grant, who realized that taking Vicksburg would be a huge tactical challenge. Political discontent in the Union made it necessary for him to try experiment after experiment to achieve a victory that would quiet the critics of Lincoln's conduct of the war.

● Look at the map on page C-149. This map is on too small a scale to give a full idea of the difficulty of the terrain. You must visualize cliffs, 200 feet high overlooking the river, and swamps, creeks, and bayous cutting the banks on both sides. Imagine you are Grant, with your troops in the north, based in Memphis. How would you set about taking Vicksburg?

Grant at first tried to move in on Vicksburg from north of the city, depending on the gunboats to support him, but he underestimated the difficulties of the terrain. In the mud and weeds of the marshy ground the attackers bogged down completely. Grant then planned to move his men downriver to a spot below the city, land them, and attack from the high ground to the south. However, he could not get his troops past the cannon commanding the river. In desperation he ordered his engineers to dig a canal to change the course of the Mississippi itself, to enable his troops to bypass the city by boat; this proved impossible.

Finally, Grant decided to make a wild gamble: he would forget about communication and supply lines, move his troops across the Mississippi, march south, recross the river below Vicksburg, then swing north and finally west to the point of attack.

► On the map on this page, trace Grant's march to outflank the city and its defenses. Roughly how many miles did his troops have to march?

For three months, in a series of five hard-fought, bloody battles, Grant's army advanced on Vicksburg. Reaching the outskirts of the city, Grant's army attacked again and again, but each time was repulsed. Grant then decided to put the city under siege. Day and night, for six weeks, Union artillery hurled shells into the stubborn city. Nearly every building was hit; many inhabitants moved into the caves along the clifftop. Food supplies fell very low; flour cost $1,000 a barrel, sugar $12 a pint measure. They say that the Vicksburg Hotel offered as its daily menu mule tail soup, boiled mule bacon, mule ham, and mule sirloin. Many of the people in the caves were reduced to eating rats.

Finally, on July 1, 1863, there was only one half-rotten biscuit apiece left for the city's weary defenders; three days later the Confederate flag was lowered. Hearing the news, Lincoln proclaimed that "The Father of Waters once more flows unvexed to the sea," and a grateful nation waited to welcome Grant to Washington.

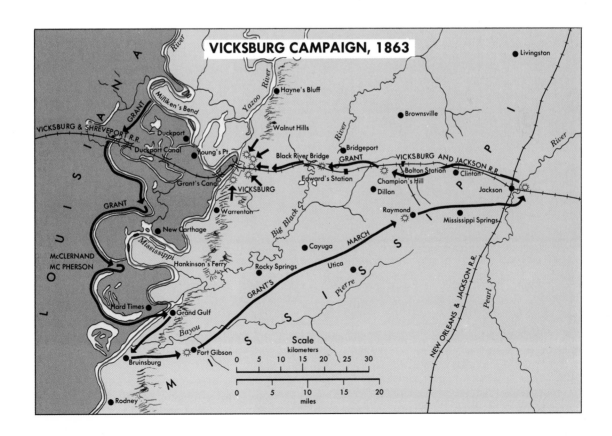

VICKSBURG CAMPAIGN, 1863

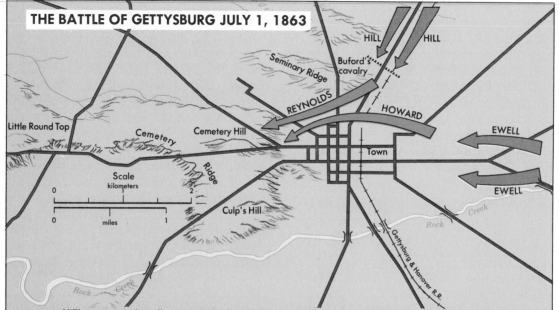

THE BATTLE OF GETTYSBURG JULY 1, 1863

Hill's men accidentally meet Buford's cavalry. Fighting begins. Reynolds's force reinforces Buford. Howard's force moves to meet Confederate force north of town. Reynolds's and Howard's forces retreat to Cemetery Hill. Meade arrives to command entire Union force. By the morning of July 2, Meade's men have established a line along Cemetery Ridge from Round Top and Little Round Top to Culp's Hill; the Confederate line is roughly parallel. Lee commands the Confederates.

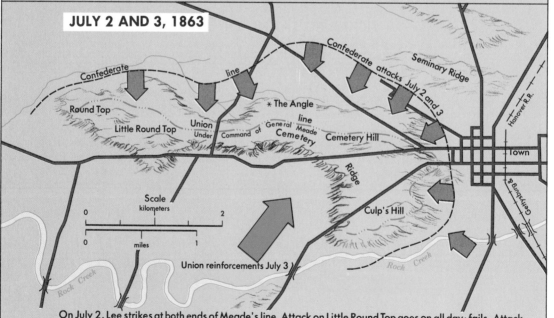

JULY 2 AND 3, 1863

On July 2, Lee strikes at both ends of Meade's line. Attack on Little Round Top goes on all day; fails. Attack on Culp's Hill also fails.

On July 3, Rebels again attack Culp's Hill; attack again fails. 15,000 Confederates drive at the entire ridge. Both Rebel flanks are smashed, but spearhead keeps pounding at the center (the Angle). Three brigades fail to smash Union line. Union reinforcements arrive and end the battle. Lee retreats to Virginia.

● Locate Vicksburg on the map. Why was the capture of Vicksburg so vital to the Union cause?

★ Can you think of any other successful sieges in history? Under what conditions is a siege likely to be successful?

● Casualties in the Vicksburg campaign were as follows: Grant's army — 1,243 killed; 7,095 wounded; Confederates — 10,000 killed and wounded; 37,000 captured. What does this suggest about Grant's qualities as a general?

★ Read more details of the Vicksburg campaign, if you are interested in military science. Find out how Grant misled the opposing generals, Pemberton and Johnston, and even President Jefferson Davis, and how Grant's tremendous energy transmitted itself to his troops and fellow generals. What calculated risks did Grant take? What happened at the five battles: Port Gibson, Raymond, Jackson, Champion's Hill, and Big Black River?

While Grant was directing the siege of Vicksburg, Lee with nearly 80,000 men was moving to meet with the Army of the Potomac. North through the Shenandoah Valley to the border of Pennsylvania the Confederates marched, followed by General Meade and a Union force. The strategy of Lee's advance into Pennsylvania was to threaten Washington, cut it off from the rest of the Union, and, if possible, defeat decisively the Army of the Potomac.

● What do you think of this strategy? Was Washington (or Richmond) vitally important? Should Lee and Davis have concentrated on the western theater — Chattanooga and Atlanta especially — rather than northern Virginia and Washington, D.C.? Explain.

In May 1863, Lee and his right-hand man, Stonewall Jackson, defeated Hooker's Troops at Chancellorsville in northern Virginia. During this battle, Stonewall Jackson was killed by the fire of his own troops.

Lee then advanced north and reached the little town of Gettysburg at the end of June. Here his advance troops bumped into Meade's forces on July 1. The greatest battle ever fought in the New World began. Neither commanding general had planned to fight here, but there they were — Lee with 76,000 men and Meade with 88,000.

► Look at the two maps on page C-150. Notice how the high ground curves like a fishhook south of the town. Which side took up a defensive position along this high ground? Was this good tactics? Notice, too, how Lee's attacks were made at all points on this position. What was the cost of such frontal attacks now that the rifle was in use?

All the first day the firing continued while both armies maneuvered for position. The Union force finally settled south of the town in a good defensive location along a three-mile line from Culp's Hill along Cemetery Ridge to two hills called Round Top and Little Round Top. To their west, along Seminary Ridge, the Confederates dug in.

Early on the second day, Lee decided to try an attack by smashing the Union left, then rolling up Cemetery Ridge, but the attempt failed. Again on July 3, Lee attacked, this time the center of the Union line. After a fierce artillery bombardment, he ordered General George E. Pickett to head straight across the valley between the ridges and up Cemetery Ridge in a desperate frontal attack with 12,000 men. Marching in perfect formation the Confederates advanced across the open field and up the slope, led by Pickett, on horseback and brandishing his sword, straight into a murderous line of fire from above. For 20 terrible minutes the two forces met and slashed with bayonets and clubbed with gun butts in hand-to-hand combat; at last the attack broke, and the Confederates had to retreat. Lee's attack had been made at a fearful cost; 80 out of every 100 men who charged the Union line fell on the bloody ground before Cemetery Ridge. On this day the tide had turned in the East; never again would Lee regain the initiative he had had before Gettysburg. On July 4, Lee retreated.

● How did Pickett's charge show the folly of the old tactics of troops advancing in formation across open ground toward an entrenched foe armed with high-powered rifles?

Thus on July 4, 1863, two great victories had been achieved by the North. The Mississippi had been conquered, and the brilliant General Lee had failed to overcome the Army of the Potomac. It was the beginning of the end. Perhaps the South should have begun peace negotiations at this point, but anger and determination on both sides seemed to make negotiations impossible.

The Character of the War Changes

By mid-1863, the character of the war had in fact changed. The objective was no longer merely to restore the Union and show the rebels the folly of secession, for in the North power was passing more and more to Radical Republicans. These were Abolitionists determined to destroy slavery and to punish the South. When the fighting was over, Senator Stewart of Nevada, in a speech in the 39th Congress, summed up the change in the war:

We commenced to force the Southern people to obey the Constitution. We said they had no right to secede. That was the first proposition. In the progress of the war it was ascertained that the negro had become an element of strength to the South . . . and President Lincoln, patriotically and properly, thank God, had the

President Lincoln visits with his generals at headquarters in Antietam, 1862

boldness to issue his proclamation and strike a blow at the war power. We then declared, and the nation's honour was pledged, that we would maintain for the negro his freedom. Then the issue became the Union and the freedom of the negro.[2]

Two years after the war, a Northern journal, *The Nation,* editorialized:

The late war was . . . a struggle between moral right and moral wrong. . . . We said that the rebellion was an immoral enterprise, conceived and carried out not by mistaken men, but by bad and unscrupulous men, animated by corrupt and selfish motives, and determined to gain their ends at whatever cost or suffering to others.

● How would such attitudes affect the conduct and outcome of the war?

★ Lincoln himself did not adopt the attitude of the Radical Republicans, although he compromised with it to some extent. Read the *Gettysburg Address,* November 19, 1863, and the *second Inaugural Address,* March 4, 1865. What did Lincoln perceive as the policy objectives of the North at this stage?

● Which was living up to Clausewitz's dictum — "War is the continuation of policy by other means" — Lincoln or the group of Radical Republicans?

The End of the War and the Final Tragedy

By the early spring of 1865, the Confederacy was collapsing. The previous November the people had elected Lincoln to another term of office. His vice-president was Andrew Johnson of Ten-

nessee. Lincoln realized that the coming years would witness bitterness between North and South. Nevertheless, he had accomplished his goal: the Union was preserved. Now an even greater United States of America could be realized.

On April 9, 1865, Robert E. Lee surrendered to General Grant at Appomattox, Virginia. Lee's hungry and shoeless men had fought as hard as they could, and Lee saw no point to continuing a struggle doomed to failure. Although some limited fighting was still taking place, the Civil War was over. Lincoln busied himself that week with plans for Reconstruction in the South. As might be expected, Lincoln's plans for the future displayed a nobility and generosity that had been evident throughout the Civil War. The South must be restored as quickly and as painlessly as possible.

★ What were the exact provisions of the surrender signed by Lee? Why do you think the terms were unusually generous?

On Good Friday the president interrupted his busy schedule for some relaxation. He and his wife went for a carriage ride and talked. They returned to the White House, dined, and then got ready to attend Ford's Theater where an amusing play, *Our American Cousin,* was being presented. While the president and the first lady watched from their box with their guests, a man arrived outside the theater. He had made certain arrangements that afternoon, and had even bored a peephole in the door of the president's box. Now, just before ten o'clock, he left his horse behind the theater and made his way to where Lincoln sat watching the comedy.

This self-appointed avenger of the defeated South was an actor named John Wilkes Booth. What negligence enabled him to reach his victim so easily no one has ever explained, but there he stood, knife and pistol in hand, at ten o'clock on

[2] *The Congressional Globe,* Thirty-Ninth Congress, first session, p. 297.

Good Friday night. In a moment he shot the president through the head, slashed a guest's arm, and sprang from the box onto the stage, shouting the motto of the state of Virginia: "Sic Semper Tyrannis!" ("Thus it is always for tyrants!") Actors and audience were momentarily paralyzed with horror, and Booth got away. Twelve days later he was surrounded. He was killed by a shot, fired either by himself or his captors. His fellow conspirators were later tried and either hanged or imprisoned.

The president was mortally wounded. He never spoke again and died before morning. The dreadful shock to the people of the Union was all the more agonizing because the tragedy came at the moment of victory, just as men and women were rejoicing that four years of slaughter and destruction were finally ending.

★ Investigate details of the Wilkes Booth plot, including the planned assassination of the cabinet members that was to take place at the same time. What happened to the other conspirators, including the innocent Mrs. Surratt?

● Look at the cartoon and poem on page C-155 from the British magazine *Punch*. Compare the earlier *Punch* cartoon, on page C-143 above. What does the comparison suggest about the change in British opinion about the Civil War? Why does the poet call himself (or

General Lee surrendered to General Grant at the Appomattox Court House in Virginia, April 9, 1865

Punch?) a "scurril jester"? Who is the mourner at the foot of the bier? What does the broken chain signify?

The tragedy of Lincoln's assassination was deeper than the mere loss of a brave, outstanding leader. It removed a man who hoped, by moderation and generosity in peace, "to bind up the nation's wounds." Worse still, it roused a wave of popular hatred for and anger against the defeated South. Lincoln's death certainly increased the influence of the Radicals in the Reconstruction of the South.

BRITANNIA SYMPATHISES WITH COLUMBIA.

Abraham Lincoln.

FOULLY ASSASSINATED, APRIL 14, 1865.

You lay a wreath on murdered LINCOLN's bier,
 You, who with mocking pencil wont to trace,
Broad for the self-complacent British sneer,
 His length of shambling limb, his furrowed face,

His gaunt, gnarled hands, his unkempt, bristling hair,
 His garb uncouth, his bearing ill at ease,
His lack of all we prize as debonair,
 Of power or will to shine, of art to please.

You, whose smart pen backed up the pencil's laugh,
 Judging each step, as though the way were plain:
Reckless, so it could point its paragraph,
 Of chief's perplexity, or people's pain.

Beside this corpse, that bears for winding-sheet
 The Stars and Stripes he lived to rear anew,
Between the mourners at his head and feet,
 Say, scurril-jester, is there room for *you?*

Yes, he had lived to shame me from my sneer,
 To lame my pencil, and confute my pen—
To make me own this hind of princes peer,
 This rail-splitter a true-born king of men.

President Andrew Johnson

4

Reconstruction, 1865-77

**More Challenges; More
Historical Controversies**

The Civil War was over. Secession was crushed. Slavery was dead. But a host of new challenges faced the nation. Southerners faced the problem of adjustment to defeat. Northern leaders faced the problem of what to do about the South. Blacks, freed at last, faced problems of adjustment: How would they make a living? How would they turn freedom into real civil and political equality?

- An important constitutional question was the status of the defeated states. Lincoln had insisted that they *never left the Union.* Radical Republicans wanted to treat them as *conquered provinces.* Why was the decision on this matter vitally significant? Consider especially state governments and representation in Congress.

- What difficulties were certain to arise from the sudden emancipation of the slaves? What difficulties would the freed men face?

- Suppose you were a Northern politician called upon to decide on policies toward the defeated South. What choices would you have made? Which priorities would you set?

1. Punish rebel leaders
2. Occupy the South with troops
3. Insist on immediate political and civil equality for blacks
4. Provide economic aid and land for ex-slaves
5. Restore regular state government in the South
6. Encourage rebels and rebel leaders to forget recent hatreds and come back into the Union on friendly and equal terms

Defend your choices. Which of the above policy objectives would be *incompatible* with one another? Why?

Quite apart from the Reconstruction of the Union and the Southern states, the period from 1865 to 1880 saw a whole new set of challenges. The westward movement, encouraged by the *Homestead Act* of 1862 and the extension of transcontinental railroads, surged forward. It brought serious clashes between Indians and the United States Army. Monetary problems, resulting from the return to gold payments, occurred. So did business crises, caused by speculation. Industry was growing faster than ever. Indeed, industry was taking new forms. The *Second Industrial Revolution* had begun. It brought new goods, new forms of energy, and vast amounts of new wealth. It also brought social problems and labor strife. Political corruption and bureaucratic corruption caused public scandals. *Chinese immigration,* dating from 1850, was a target for racial prejudice and riots. All these turbulent developments coincided with the stress and strain of the postwar Reconstruction period.

A period so hectic naturally invites divergent historical interpretations. Southern sympathizers have seen the period as *The Tragic Era*[1]: a time when Southern whites were driven to needless bitterness and when race relations in the South were worsened rather than improved. Such sympathizers claim that Northern people and politicians were hypocritical in trying to force on the South racial, political, and economic equality, while the North was quite unwilling to accept that equality in its own farms and factories and governments. Those who condemn the Reconstruction policies also point out that it left national politics and Southern state politics distorted for a hundred years; the South remained a *one-party region*. On the other hand, *revisionist* historians have asserted that Reconstruction policies were necessary to break the hold of slavery on the South and to give blacks the chance to acquire dignity and responsibility. They claim that Radical Republicans were far from hypocritical, that they were sincerely dedicated to freedom and equality, and that their failure lay in not pushing Reconstruction through to its completion. Revisionists also point to the social improvements of the Reconstruction era: tax-supported schools and rebuilt railroads, for example.

★ You will have to make your own mind up about these historical controversies. Here are two important books that attack Reconstruction: Claude G. Bowers, *The Tragic Era* (1929) and Hodding Carter, *The Angry Scar* (1959). And here are two revisionist books that defend it: Kenneth M. Stampp, *The Era of Reconstruction* (1964) and John Hope Franklin, *Reconstruction:*

---

[1]The title of Claude G. Bowers's book on Reconstruction, published in 1929.

A cartoon on Reconstruction

After the Civil War (1961). Another recent defense of congressional Reconstruction is W. R. Brock, *An American Crisis: Congress and Reconstruction* (1963). Very interesting is a short study of changing opinions about the Negroes' future: James M. McPherson, "The Antislavery Legacy: From Reconstruction to the NAACP," in Barton J. Bernstein (ed.), *Towards a New Past: Dissenting Essays in American History* (1967).

The New President: Andrew Johnson

The death of Abraham Lincoln left a dreadful gap in the national government. His successor, Andrew Johnson, was not quite the man to lead the Union firmly. He was born in North Carolina. After an impoverished childhood, he moved to eastern Tennessee where he worked as a tailor. He taught himself to read, and it was not until he was in his 20's that he learned how to write. Johnson's success in politics was phenomenal: alderman, mayor, governor, and finally, United States senator. When South Carolina left the Union, he alone among the Southern legislators urged Congress to use force to prevent secession. Although a Democrat, Johnson was nominated vice-president in 1864 by the Republicans because of his Southern background and loyalist Union views. Just 41 days after the inauguration of Lincoln, Andrew Johnson became president of the United States.

● Why were the Radical Republicans—men who wanted to punish the defeated South—at first glad to see this former Tennessee senator replace Lincoln as president?

● What disadvantages might a president from Tennessee have in leading a Congress of Northerners?

Thaddeus Stevens

Charles Sumner

Johnson Versus the Radical Republicans

During the summer of 1865, while Congress was in recess, Johnson proceeded to carry out a Reconstruction plan similar to that proposed by Lincoln. Based on the theory that the Southern states had never left the Union, the presidential plan provided for a *general amnesty* and restoration of property. In any state, people who took an oath of allegiance to the federal government were allowed to elect a convention for the purpose of organizing a state government which would be recognized by the president. By December, all of the seceded states—except Texas—had complied with Johnson's plan and had representatives, mostly former Confederates, waiting to take their seats in Congress. Alexander Stephens, former vice-president of the Confederacy, was among those elected. The Radical Republicans—headed by Senator Charles Sumner and Representative Thaddeus Stevens—were enraged. They refused to seat the Southerners until a committee could investigate if any of the "so-called Confederate states . . . were entitled to be represented in Congress . . ." The Radical Republicans were not prepared to forget the bloody Civil War so quickly.

The situation was made especially awkward for Johnson, because the new state governments in the South acted very foolishly. They had to accept the abolition of slavery under the *Thirteenth Amendment* (ratified December 1865). However, state after state adopted so-called *Black Codes,* which were designed to keep the black people in a condition of subordination and inferiority. Moreover, Southerners who sympathized with the Union were harshly discriminated against in government and business. Leaders of the rebellion were elected into key positions. Senator Ben Wade wrote to Sumner, in July 1865:

The President is pursuing . . . a course in regard to reconstruction that can result in nothing but consigning the great Union, or Republican party, bound hand and foot, to the tender mercies of the rebels we have so lately conquered in the field and their copperhead allies in the north.[2]

- How did the new state governments in the South play right into the hands of Northern Radicals? Could they have been smarter? How? Were the Radicals justified in rejecting Southern representatives?

- When the Germans were defeated in 1945 they repudiated the regime of Hitler and its ideology. How does this attitude compare with the defeated South in 1865?

★ Study an example of a *Black Code* (that of Mississippi is an extreme example). What did it say about blacks' rights to own property, to marry whites, to leave their jobs, to be unemployed, to possess arms? What happened to a Negro who could not pay a fine? What provision was made for Negroes under 18 who lacked the means of support?

- A Radical, Henry Wilson, said of the code of Mississippi: it "makes the freed men the slaves of society." Do you agree? Explain.

The Radicals Take Over

The era of Radical Reconstruction began in April of 1866 with the controversy over the *Fourteenth Amendment.* The amendment was aimed at preventing state legislatures from taking away the rights of black citizens. Here are some of the provisions of the Fourteenth Amendment:

1. All persons born or naturalized in the United States are citizens of

---

[2]Quoted in W. R. Brock, *op. cit.,* p. 42.

the United States and of the state they live in.

2. No state can take away the rights of citizens of the United States.

3. If a state prevents some of its citizens (blacks, of course) from voting in elections, it shall have fewer representatives in Congress.

4. Persons who rebelled against the United States cannot hold political office in the United States, or any state, unless Congress by a two-thirds vote permits them to do so.

5. The United States will not pay off any of the debts of the Confederacy.

The ex-rebel states were staggered: 10 out of 11 states refused to ratify the Fourteenth Amendment.[3] They were joined by Maryland, Kentucky, and Delaware, which viewed the proposed amendment as infringing on states' rights. (The president and many Northerners shared this view). The amendment was defeated, but only temporarily. The Radicals waited for the November congressional elections. It was in connection with these elections that President Johnson made a political blunder. Not until August of 1866—three months before the important elections—did Johnson try to organize his supporters as a political force under the label of the National Union party, which was the name the Republicans had adopted in 1864 for the Lincoln-Johnson campaign. It was a hopeless effort. The Radicals won control of both houses of Congress and were strong enough to override any presidential veto. They were now able to break the control of former rebels in the Southern states.

★ One of the first clashes between Johnson and the Radicals involved the Freedmen's Bureau. Investigate its functions. Why did Johnson view it as an unconstitutional organization?

● One of the ways by which the Radicals insured their success in the election of 1866 was by "waving the bloody shirt." What does this expression mean?

● What elements of the Fourteenth Amendment caused the advocates of states' rights to come out against the amendment? How were the Radicals able to use this opposition to their own favor during the elections of 1866?

● Why were many whites, in the North as well as in the South, opposed to the Fourteenth Amendment and the Freedmen's Bureau?

The Reconstruction Act of 1867 and the Fourteenth Amendment

To force the South to ratify the Fourteenth Amendment, Congress in March of 1867 passed two *Reconstruction Acts* over Johnson's veto. They swept away the rebel-controlled Southern state governments that had been recognized by Johnson. They grouped the former Confederate states (except Tennessee) into five military districts, each headed by an army general. They set up martial law enforced by federal troops. And they ordered conventions to establish new state governments. The Southern states were to be readmitted to the Union only after they ratified the Fourteenth Amendment. Military occupation put a stop to the oppression of the freed blacks.

★ Read the Fourteenth Amendment. Which parts of it are of purely historical interest? Which are of great constitutional importance today?

● It is often said that Section 1 of the

---

[3]Tennessee was the one former Confederate state that ratified the amendment.

The Freedmen's Bureau brought education to black people for the first time

Fourteenth Amendment reversed (or was intended to reverse) the traditional relationship of the national government and the state governments toward the rights of individual persons. Explain this statement.

● Ratification of the amendment called for approval by the legislatures of three-fourths of the states. In 1868 there were 37 states, of which 29 ratified. Although Ohio and New Jersey withdrew their ratifications, Congress ruled that they could not legally do so. Would the Fourteenth Amendment have been ratified without the Reconstruction Acts? Is it fair to say that the Radical Republicans tried to keep within the Constitution while breaking it? Is it also fair to say that the amendment was and is so important that it justified the political devices that made it part of the Constitution? Explain.

● How did the Reconstruction Acts show that Congress rejected the Lincoln-Johnson theory that the rebel states had never left the Union?

The "Black Reconstruction" Governments in the South

Late in 1867, conventions were elected in the Southern states. They were elected under military supervision. Anyone who had taken part in the Civil War on the Confederate side was not allowed to vote. Radicals controlled the conventions, and many blacks participated. In the South Carolina convention, Negroes were the majority. New constitutions were drawn up. These constitutions protected the civil rights of black people, and denied political rights to ex-rebels. Between 1868 and 1870, Congress approved the new constitutions. In the Southern states, governments were elected. These Reconstruction governments operated under the protection of military forces for several years. The last federal troops were withdrawn in 1877.

At first the Reconstruction state governments were controlled by Radicals. Many Afro-Americans were members of the state legislatures. What is the verdict of history on these Reconstruction governments?

There are two very different versions. One is the Southern version, which was accepted for many years. It argues that the governments were unrepresentative, since many whites were not allowed to vote or hold office. It claims that the governments were run by a mixture of *carpetbaggers* (politicians from the North), *scalawags* (Southerners who collaborated with Northerners), and blacks who were inexperienced in politics. The Southern horror version further emphasizes the extravagance and corruption of the Reconstruction governments. State debts and taxes certainly shot up. In Louisiana, for ex-

Blanche K. Bruce was elected United States Senator from Mississippi in 1880

ample, the state debt went from $11 million in 1868 to $50 million in 1875. In the same period, taxes were multiplied five times. In the same period, the state debt in Arkansas went from $3½ million to nearly $16 million.

The South had an interest in keeping up the horror version. However, recent historians have challenged it. Not all Reconstruction governments were dishonest, and, in any case, national and Northern state and city governments were pretty scandalous during this period. Moreover, governments in the South could not avoid heavy expenses. There was much physical rebuilding to be done. Tax-supported education had to be established. Hospitals had to be set up. Many buildings had to be rebuilt. Above all, railroads were needed, and much state money was used to subsidize railroad construction.

Apart from these things, *revisionist* historians point out that the Reconstruction governments *did* give the vote to poor whites and to blacks. Both these groups lost the vote soon after the Reconstruction period ended. Moreover, one great national

Section 1 of the Fourteenth Amendment

All persons born or naturalized in the United States, and subject to the jurisdiction thereof, are citizens of the United States and of the State wherein they reside. No State shall make or enforce any law which shall abridge the privileges or immunities of citizens of the United States; nor shall any State deprive any person of life, liberty, or property, without due process of law; nor deny to any person within its jurisdiction the equal protection of the laws.

benefit remained from Reconstruction: the Fourteenth and Fifteenth Amendments. Although these were largely ignored from 1876 until the 1930's, they became the basis of the civil rights revolution in the 1950's and '60s.

Above all the Southern blacks did improve their condition during Reconstruction. Many learned to read. It has been estimated that 600,000 Negroes were in public schools by 1877. Many were helped by the Freedmen's Bureau and by Northern religious and philanthropic organizations, which sent representatives to help on the spot. Many of the teachers who helped were "carpetbaggers."

● The South was a devastated and underdeveloped region c. 1865. How does this fact account in part for the problems and reputation of the Reconstruction governments?

● Ought the national government to have supplied massive funds to revive the South's economy and improve the lives of the blacks? How could the money have been spent?

● Read the Fifteenth Amendment. How does it reinforce the Fourteenth?

The Fifteenth Amendment

Section 1. The right of citizens of the United States to vote shall not be denied or abridged by the United States or by any State on account of race, color, or previous condition of servitude —

Section 2. The Congress shall have power to enforce this article by appropriate legislation —

Soldiers in captured Ku Klux Klan uniforms, 1868

Southern Reaction

Frustrated and angry Southerners resorted to terror and violence. Underground organizations, like the Ku Klux Klan, were started. The Klan and other secret societies sought to prevent the freed slaves from voting. Blacks who resisted were beaten, shot, and hanged. Equally successful was the threat of economic pressure. The war had freed the Negroes, but they were still laborers. Planters refused to rent land to blacks, employers refused to give them work, and storekeepers refused them credit.

● What might the Radicals have done to prevent economic pressure from robbing the freed blacks of their rights? Why did they not do anything effective?

Opening of the high court of impeachment in the Senate for the trial of Andrew Johnson, 1868

● Were the freed blacks caught in a power struggle between Northern Radicals and local (embittered) white majorities? Explain.

★ Investigate the Ku Klux Klan of 1867 and the one founded in 1915. In what ways were they similar? In what ways did they differ? How widespread is the Ku Klux Klan today?

The President on Trial

Radical Republicans were in control of Congress in 1868. Yet President Johnson continued to resist their Reconstruction policies as far as he was able. The Radical leaders decided to try to remove the president.

As part of their campaign against Johnson, the Radicals passed a *Tenure of Office Act* in 1867. This act required the president to obtain Senate approval before he *dismissed* any members of his cabinet or other high officials.

● Why did Johnson object to the Tenure of Office Act? Did it imply a revolution in the American Constitution? Explain.

The Radicals knew that Johnson was trying to get rid of Secretary of War Edwin Stanton, who acted as an informer for the Radicals. Since Stanton had been appointed by Lincoln, Johnson saw no reason why he could not dismiss him. Soon after Stanton's dismissal, the House voted to impeach Johnson for such "high crimes and misdemeanors" as breaking the Tenure of Office Act, and ten other less serious actions.

The trial, presided over by Chief Justice Salmon P. Chase, lasted several months. By the time the decisive vote on acquittal or conviction was to be taken, it became apparent that six Republicans were going to join with the Democrats in voting to acquit. The vote of freshman Radical Edmund Ross of Kansas was needed to save Johnson. His name was called. "I al-

THE PAROQUET OF THE WH—E HO—E.

A cartoon of President Johnson

most literally looked down into my open grave," he recalled. "Friendships, position, fortune, everything that makes life desirable to an ambitious man were about to be swept away by the breath of my mouth, perhaps forever." Senator Ross's decision to vote "Not guilty" saved President Johnson.

- Read the sections of the Constitution dealing with impeachment:
    Article I, Section 2, clause 5;
    Article I, Section 3, clauses 6 and 7;
    Article II, Section 4.
    What is the purpose of including impeachment in the Constitution? Who votes impeachment charges? Who tries persons impeached? What are the penalties if the impeached person is voted guilty?

- Should impeachment be used to remove a president with whose policies two-thirds of the members of Congress disagree? Explain.

★ Johnson's term of office was not entirely a failure. Investigate the details of the enforcement of the Monroe Doctrine, as it applied to Archduke Maximilian of Mexico and Napoleon III of France, and the purchase of Alaska from Russia in 1867.

The End of Radicalism and Reconstruction

Johnson's successor to the presidency was Civil War hero Ulysses S. Grant. Under Grant, Congress dominated the national scene, and the presidency lost even more authority and prestige. So low did its power fall, that in 1885 a future president, Woodrow Wilson, wrote a scathing book called *Congressional Government,* denouncing the confusion and irresponsibility that ensued when the real power in America was divided between the chairmen of congressional committees.

- Why may the domination of policy by Congress and its various committees produce political confusion, lack of clear direction, irresponsibility, and corruption? Why did the Constitutional Convention design a one-man executive?

★ Would you say the presidency or Congress is the stronger branch today? Explain.

During Grant's presidency, the Reconstruction governments continued to function in most Southern states, but their character changed. They were largely dependent for their existence on federal troops and militia. Gradually these forces were withdrawn. The Ku Klux Klan continued its campaign of terror. Democrats began to regain control in Southern states. In spite of certain achievements, and in spite of their work for the freedmen, the Reconstruction governments were obviously failing. Perhaps the Radical Republicans hoped for too much too quickly. Perhaps they failed to give adequate economic aid. Millions of ex-slaves could not be converted in ten years into literate voters, or successful politicians, farmers, and businessmen.

By the mid-1870's, Northern enthusiasm for Reconstruction was fading fast. Even former Abolitionists began to talk about the mistaken policies of *immediatism*—that is, the policies of raising the blacks to complete equality and freedom in a few years. The revolutionary fervor faded. People began to feel that the South had been sufficiently punished. Moreover, corruption at all levels of government caused many to lose any idealistic feeling about politics. So the experiment of Reconstruction fizzled out, apparently a failure, leaving feelings of bitter indignation in the South, feelings of betrayal and helplessness among Southern Negroes, and a mixture of guilt and disillusion in the North. The old racist forces returned to power in the Southern states.

● Would you say Reconstruction was a complete failure? Explain.

● How might Reconstruction have intensified white racism in the South?

● Racial prejudice against blacks was widespread in the North. How would this affect Reconstruction in the South?

● Comment on James Truslow Adams's epigram: "The war left the South prostrate; Reconstruction left it maddened."

● Public opinion in democratic nations tends to be wayward and erratic. If a policy is not successfully completed during a certain period, it will almost certainly collapse or fade away and maybe even be replaced by an exactly opposite policy. Does the history of Reconstruction support this generalization? Can you give other illustrations?

The disillusion of Northerners was vividly expressed by a carpetbagger Abolitionist from Ohio, Albion Tourgee. His words may serve as the epitaph of an idealistic experiment that somehow lost its way.

We tried to superimpose the civilization, the idea of the North, upon the South at a moment's warning. We presumed, that, by the suppression of rebellion, the Southern white man had become identical with the Caucasian of the North in thought and sentiment; and that the slave, by emancipation, had become a saint and a Solomon at once. So we tried to build up communities there which should be identical in thought, sentiment, growth, and development, with those of the North. It was a Fool's Errand.

Johnson is not guilty

(Left) Walt Whitman

(Right) Samuel Clemens (Mark Twain)

5

Toward the Last Frontier

A Contradictory Decade

The depravity of the business classes of our country is not less than has been supposed, but infinitely greater. The official services of America, national, state, and municipal, in all their branches and departments, except the judiciary, are saturated in corruption, bribery, falsehood, mal-administration; and the judiciary is tainted. The great cities reek with respectable as much as non-respectable robbery and scoundrelism.[1]

So wrote the poet of American democracy, Walt Whitman, six years after the end of the Civil War. He was not alone in his shock and revulsion; for corruption was not confined to the Reconstruction governments of the South; it seeped through the life of the Northern and Western sections of the nation.

Corruption was perhaps encouraged by economic instability. The 1870's were a strangely confusing time. The South was still crippled by the aftereffects of war. The rest of the country suffered a serious *depression,* from 1873 to 1878. There was much unemployment. There were strikes and violence. Yet along with the depression there was economic expansion. More railroads were built. Pioneers were settling on the Great Plains. Cattlemen brought great herds of cattle from the Southwest to the markets of the Northeast. Fresh beef and wheat bread—formerly expensive luxuries—were now available to ordinary working people. New inventions improved agricultural efficiency—barbed wire, reapers and harvesters, steel plows, and threshing machines. The supply of pork, too, increased as the corn belt was settled and exploited.

Other inventions changed men's lives. The war had expanded Northern industry and brought many applications of standardization and mass production. Clothing, shoes, canned food, many tools, and much equipment were in abundant supply. New processes enabled a vast steel industry, centered in Pittsburgh, to grow. Coal and oil and iron ore were exploited. Vast supplies of lumber were available on the Pacific coast. The great cities of America grew, the nerve centers of the new industrial society. Bankers and financiers supplied the funds for unprecedented economic development. Great fortunes were made by men who had started life in poverty and hardship.

● Do you think there may be a connection between the corruption in politics and business and the exuberant economic and pioneering expansion of the 1870's and succeeding decades? Explain.

---

[1] Walt Whitman, *Democratic Vistas* (published 1871), quoted in Avery Craven, Walter Johnson, and F. Roger Dunn (eds.), *A Documentary History of the American People* (Boston: Ginn, 1951), pp. 473–74.

- Why did the war stimulate production of goods like ready-made clothes and boots, canned food, standardized tools, and guns?

- One of the big problems of the United States from the 1870's until the 1910's was the *farm problem.* Part of this problem was that the price of farm products could not keep up with the price of industrial goods. How did this affect the farmers' standard of living? Can you see why the prices of the two types of goods would tend to become unbalanced?

- Industrial goods were *protected* by *high tariffs.* How did this affect prices?

- A period of rapid economic growth generally leads to *financial speculation.* What general social consequences may result from excessive speculation?

- Many persons profited from the booming economy and the growth of cities. What groups or classes in society might suffer from economic insecurity, poor wages, and poor housing during a period of expansion and speculation? Why?

President Ulysses S. Grant

To succeed Andrew Johnson, the Republicans picked a military hero, General Grant. The congressional Radicals had, to all intents and purposes, gained supreme control in government. They calculated that the general would agree with their views. They were right. Ulysses S. Grant was a good man, but he lacked, perhaps, a tough knowledge of the realities of politics. Though he himself was honest,

(Left) Shooting buffalo from the Kansas-Pacific railroad trains

(Right) Edwin L. Drake brought in the first oil well in America. It was drilled near Titusville, Pennsylvania in 1859

Grant seemed to know little about the temptations of politics, especially when dealing with unscrupulous politicians. He was apt to remain loyal to his friends even after they had proved dishonest or incapable of doing their jobs. This was the beginning of the "Gilded Age" — an age of shoddy opulence and rapid fortune making. President Grant never quite understood what was going on.

The Presidential Elections of 1868 and 1872

Presidential Election, 1868

	Popular Vote	Electoral Vote
Ulysses S. Grant (Rep.)	3,013,000	214
Horatio Seymour (Dem.)	2,703,000	80

How the states went:

Grant carried 25 states

Seymour carried only 8: New York, New Jersey, Delaware, Maryland, Georgia, Louisiana, Kentucky, and Oregon

Three unreconstructed states did not take part: Virginia, Mississippi, and Texas

Presidential Election, 1872

	Popular Vote	Electoral Vote
Ulysses S. Grant (Rep.)	3,597,000	292
Horace Greeley (Dem. and Liberal Rep.)	2,834,000	74*

(Two minor candidates also ran)

*Greeley died between the election and the meeting of the electoral college; his electoral vote was divided among several persons

Grant carried all states except Georgia, Kentucky, Louisiana, Maryland, Missouri, Tennessee, Texas

A burden Grant had to shoulder

● The term *Gilded Age* was apparently invented by Mark Twain and Charles Dudley Warner, who collaborated on a satirical novel with that title. What does the phrase suggest? Was it appropriate?

Eight Years of Scandal

Grant's two terms in office were notorious for scandals. In 1869, for instance, two speculators decided to buy up all available gold, drive up its price, and then sell it at a tremendous profit. To "corner" the gold market, James Fisk and Jay Gould had to be certain that the government would not release its own gold reserves. Involved in the intended swindle were the sister and brother-in-law of Grant. The public came to find out about the plot, and the president released $4 million of government gold on the market, thus foiling the conspiracy. Many speculators were ruined.

An even more bizarre scandal occurred the following year. The dictator of the Dominican Republic, a small nation in the Caribbean, informed Grant that he was willing to sell his country to the United States. The president dispatched his personal secretary to work out a treaty, as well as warships to protect the dictator's life. When the Senate refused to go along with anything so underhanded, Grant himself lobbied in the Senate corridors. If only his plan had been adopted, Grant said, the recently freed blacks might have been deported to a rich, new country of their own. The Senate, nevertheless, refused to ratify the treaty, and the scheme came to nothing.

Corruption was not confined to the executive branch. It was prevalent in the legislative branch as well. The worst example was, perhaps, the *Crédit Mobilier* affair in 1872. The Crédit Mobilier construction company was an illegal device set up by owners of stock in the Union Pacific Railroad. The idea was to take profits from the railroad company and pay them to the stockholders of the Crédit Mobilier. In order to stop Congress from investigating this dishonest business, the promoters gave large amounts of shares to leading congressmen. The conspiracy was exposed by the New York *Sun* newspaper.

Part of the Republican party split away in 1872. Its members were angered by corruption. They also resented the Reconstruction policy in the South. They formed the Liberal Republican party and nominated Horace Greeley, editor of the *New York Tribune*, to run against Grant. The Democrats also nominated Greeley, not because they liked him, but to try to defeat Grant. However, Grant was re-elected, and the succession of scandals resumed.

★ Investigate some of the other scandals of the Grant era:

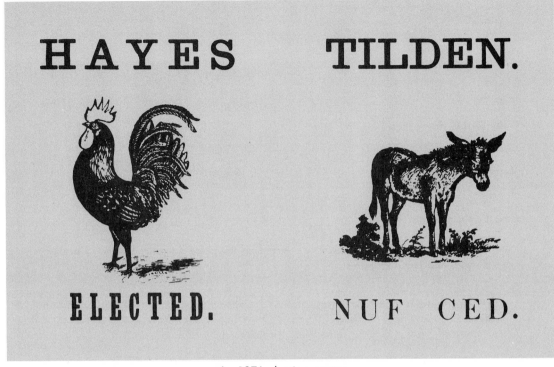

An 1876 election poster

1. The Tweed Ring of New York City, broken up by Samuel J. Tilden;
2. Thomas Murphy and the New York Custom House Scandal;
3. The St. Louis "Whisky Ring" scandal of 1875;
4. General William Belknap and the Bureau of Indian Affairs scandal.

★ One bright achievement in Grant's administration was the *Alabama arbitration*. What was that?

The Disputed Election of 1876

Although Grant indicated a willingness to accept a third term in office, the Republican political experts realized that the American public had had enough of the widespread graft and corruption. The nation, having been hit with a depression in 1873, wanted a change in leadership. In convention, the Republicans chose as their candidate Rutherford B. Hayes, an honest politician who had served three terms as governor of Ohio. Aware that the issue of the campaign would be reform, the Democrats nominated Governor Samuel J. Tilden of New York, who had been responsible for crushing the Tweed Ring. In the popular vote, Tilden received about 200,000 votes more than Hayes; but it is the electoral vote that determines the winner in presidential contests, and that was where the problem lay.

The electoral votes from four states were doubtful. In Oregon, the Democratic governor illegally appointed one Democratic elector, although the Republicans clearly won that state. A much more difficult issue was raised in three Southern states: South Carolina, Florida, and Louisiana. Here Democrats intimidated Republican voters, and Republican Reconstruction governments in return "threw out"

The Presidential Election of 1876

Final Returns

	Popular Vote	Electoral Vote
Rutherford B. Hayes (Rep.)	4,034,000	185
Samuel J. Tilden (Dem.)	4,285,000	184
Minor candidates	92,500	

How the states went:

Hayes received the vote of 21 states (including the disputed votes of South Carolina, Florida, and Louisiana)

Tilden carried 17 states: Arkansas, Alabama, Connecticut, Delaware, Georgia, Indiana, Kentucky, Maryland, Mississippi, Missouri, New Jersey, New York, North Carolina, Tennessee, Texas, Virginia, and West Virginia

many Democratic votes on the grounds that they were invalid. As a result, two separate sets of election returns came from each of these states.

To make matters worse, the votes of the four states were absolutely crucial. Together, they had 22 electoral votes. Without those 22 votes, the electoral college was divided into 184 votes for Tilden, and 163 for his opponent. To win, one candidate had to have 185 votes.

● If all the 22 disputed ballots had been thrown out, neither candidate would have received a majority of electoral votes. Bearing in mind that the Democrats controlled the House and the Republicans the Senate, who would have been chosen to succeed Grant?

Outbreaks of violence seemed likely in the South. Congress created an electoral commission consisting of five senators (3 Republicans, 2 Democrats); five representatives (3 Democrats, 2 Republicans); and five members of the Supreme Court (2 Democrats, 2 Republicans, and a fifth member to be chosen by these four). The sole independent (nonparty) member of the Court was chosen. However, this justice was elected to the Senate. He therefore resigned and was replaced by a Republican. On March 2, 1877, by a vote of 8 to 7, the commission awarded all 22 disputed ballots to Hayes. It was a straight party decision. Hayes was declared president by one electoral vote.

★ What are some of the main arguments that have been put forth in favor of the electoral college system? What arguments have been made to abolish it? Where did the idea of the electoral college originate? Why was this device included in the Constitution?

With the election of Rutherford B. Hayes, the Reconstruction experiment ended. The North was weary and had lost enthusiasm for the cause. Moreover, it seems that Hayes agreed to withdraw the few remaining federal troops from the South to soften the bitterness of the disputed election. The troops were withdrawn a month after his inauguration. The people of the United States could now concentrate on the business of exploiting the resources of their land. Southern states were able to restore the system of white supremacy. Hayes's presidency was unmarked by scandal or major crises, although there were some labor troubles. There were also scandals in the New York State Republican party—scandals that Hayes repudiated and fought.

★ What was the *Greenback Labor movement?* Who were the *Molly Maguires?*

★ What was the scandal in New York, associated with Senator Roscoe Conkling and Chester A. Arthur? How did it give rise to the *Stalwart* faction, and what part did the Stalwarts play in trying to nominate Grant once more in 1880?

The Last Frontier

Today, there are new frontiers in Alaska and maybe elsewhere. However, in the latter half of the nineteenth century, the Great Plains, which became the breadbasket of America, was the last great frontier. The rush of railroaders, cattlemen, and homesteaders on to the Great Plains was part and parcel of the speculative, exploitive atmosphere of the time. The Civil

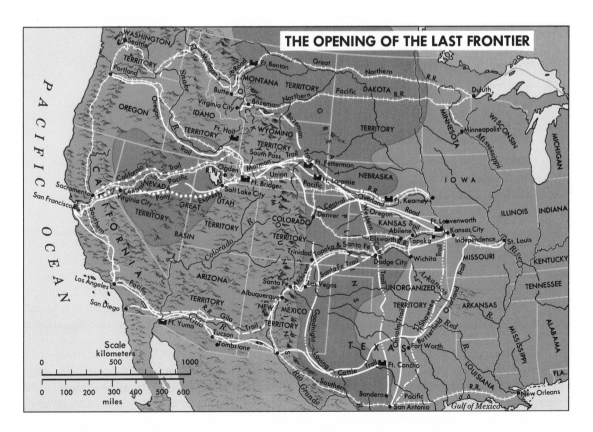

INDIANS OF THE PLAINS AND THE SOUTHWEST

War and the hopes and irritations of Reconstruction faded. A new era of power and turbulence was beginning.

The opening up of the Great Plains—once called the "Great American Desert"—brought a final tragic clash between the Indians and the settlers. In the East, after a trail of broken treaties, the tribes had long been crushed and their survivors herded into reservations in Oklahoma. The Indians of the Pacific areas had been largely wiped out or driven out. But in the true desert between the Sierra Nevada and the Rockies, and on the great grassy Plains, more than 200,000 Indians survived in freedom. Those of the Great Plains were nomadic hunters, dependent on the vast herds of wild buffalo for food, clothing, tents, and fuel. The names of these peoples are part of the romantic heritage of America. On the Plains were Sioux, or Dakota; Cheyenne, Comanche,

Blackfoot, Arapaho, and Kiowa. In the desert Southwest lived the Apache, the Navajo and the Pueblo; and in the Rockies the Ute. Much of their land had already been seized by the government or by white settlers.

The Destruction of the Indians

The story of the wars that drove the remnants of the Indian peoples into reservations is confused and ugly. It includes many brutal surprise attacks by both Indians and whites — attacks in which women and children were massacred. It includes ghastly atrocities by both sides: scalpings, torture, and shocking mutilation of the dead and wounded.

► Look at the map on page C-176. Note the location of various Indian peoples. Note how they had been driven inward from the East and West as the frontier of white settlement moved forward.

► Look at the chart on page C-178. Roughly how many serious episodes of violence can you count?

● Do you think that the Indians had any serious hope of maintaining their own way of life of free hunting on the Plains? Why or why not? What were some disadvantages of the Indians when faced with state militia or infantry, cavalry, and artillery of the U. S. Army?

● Look at the following quotations. What do they suggest about the nature of the clash between Indians and white men?

1. U.S. Commissioner James Steele talking to Cheyenne and Arapaho chiefs in 1865, after the Sand Creek massacre. He is explaining why the Indians must leave Colorado and go on to a reservation south of the Arkansas River.

We all fully realize that it is hard for any people to leave their homes and graves of their ancestors, but, unfortunately for you, gold has been discovered in your country, and a crowd of white people have gone there to live, and a great many of these people are the worst enemies of the Indians — men who do not care for their interests, and who would not stop at any crime to enrich themselves. These men are now in your country — in all parts of it — and there is no portion where you can live and maintain yourselves but what you will come in contact with them. The consequences of this state of things are that you are in constant danger of being imposed upon, and you have to resort to arms in self-defense. Under the circumstances, there is, in the opinion of the commission, no part of the former country large enough where you can live in peace.[2]

2. Red Cloud, chief of the Oglala Sioux, speaking to U.S. commissioners at Fort Laramie in June 1866. He is protesting against the forcible opening of a road through the Powder River country in Wyoming and the Dakotas.

The white men have crowded the Indians back year by year . . . until we are forced to live in a small country north of the Platte, and now our last hunting ground, the home of the People, is to be taken from us. Our women and children will starve, but for my part I prefer to die fighting rather than by starva-

[2]Quoted in Dee Brown, *Bury My Heart at Wounded Knee: An Indian History of the American West* (New York: Bantam, 1972), pp. 97–8.

Indian Wars, c. 1850-86

1849-59	Indians of California wiped out or banished.
1863-64	Defeat of the Navajos, who were later (1868) allowed to settle on a reservation in northern Arizona.
1862-71	War with the Apaches ends temporarily with forced settlement on reservations. Later, Geronimo led a long guerrilla rebellion.
1851	Treaty at Fort Laramie: Indians guarantee the safety of white travelers on the Oregon Trail.
1854-55	War: Gen. Harney raids Sioux at Blue Water Creek.
1857	War with the Cheyennes (Nebraska and Kansas).
1862	Ferocious war in Minnesota with Little Crow's Santee Sioux, who were finally defeated, but joined the Teton Sioux.
1864	After an armistice agreement, Colonel Chivington with Colorado militia massacred 300 Indians at Sand Creek, eastern Colorado.
1864-65	General Indian war along the Platte rivers. The trouble died down for a time.
1866-68	War with Red Cloud and the Oglala Sioux over the Bozeman Trail and the Union Pacific in Wyoming. Captain Fetterman and 80 men were ambushed and killed. In 1868 the U.S. government gave up the trail: treaty signed at Fort Laramie.
1868	Custer surprises and kills many survivors of the Sand Creek massacre (Black Kettle's Cheyennes) on the Washita River. This was part of General Sheridan's plan to crush the Cheyennes.
1868-71	Sheridan continues policy of exterminating and terrorizing Cheyennes and Apaches.
1874-75	Custer breaks the "treaty" with Red Cloud by invading the Black Hills of South Dakota. Gold was discovered. Indians ordered to reservations.
1876	Federal troops invade the territory of the Northern Cheyennes and Sioux. Crazy Horse's Cheyennes defeat Crook's troops at Rosebud Creek. Custer and 225 cavalry were defeated and wiped out at Little Bighorn by Sioux and Cheyennes under Crazy Horse, Sitting Bull, and Gall.
1877	The Indian alliance dissolves. Crazy Horse defeated and killed. Chief Joseph and his Nez Percé rounded up in Montana.
1878	Northern Cheyennes break out of reservation in Oklahoma; they were pursued and defeated.
1879	Rebellion of Utes in Colorado put down.
1886	Geronimo's protracted guerrilla Apache raids were finally put down.
1890	The Ghost Dance — last symbol of Indian resistance — suppressed. Sitting Bull and his Sioux were massacred at Wounded Knee, South Dakota. The last frontier was closed in the same year.

(Left) Chief Sitting Bull of the Sioux; (Above) at the Battle of Little Big Horn, "General" Custer and his troops were wiped out by Chief Sitting Bull and his Indians.

tion. . . . Great Father sends us presents and wants new road. But White Chief goes with soldiers to steal road before Indian says yes or no!³

3. **General Winfield Scott Hancock speaking to Cheyenne chiefs at Pawnee Creek, 1867.**

"The white man is coming out here so fast that nothing can stop him," Hancock boasted. "Coming from the East, and coming from the West, like a prairie on fire in a high wind. Nothing can stop him. The reason for it is, that the whites are a numerous people, and they are spreading out. They require room and cannot help it. Those on one sea in the West wish to communicate with those living on another sea in the East, and that is the reason they are building these roads, these wagon roads and railroads, and telegraphs. . . . You must not let your young men stop them; you must keep your men off the roads. . . . I have no more to say. I will await the end of your council, to see whether you want war or peace."⁴

★ Anthropologists would probably label the basic phenomenon of the Indian wars as a case of *culture contact* leading to *culture conflict*. What does this mean? What were the main conflicting factors in relations

---

³*Ibid.*, p. 125.

⁴*Ibid.*, pp. 147–48.

between Indians and whites? Consider: economic system, social organization, technology, values.

● By about 1871 the U. S. government had apparently concluded that the only feasible policy was to concentrate the Indians in reservations, taking away most of their traditional lands or hunting grounds. What alternative policies might have been tried?

★ Read about some of the incidents listed in the chart on page C-178. Did the U.S. government follow a clear, consistent policy? Did it use its vastly superior force intelligently and humanely? Explain. Can you find evidence of confusion of policy between local settlers or railroaders, territorial or state authorities, local U.S. Army commanders, and officials in Washington?

★ What is *genocide?* Would you call the U.S. government's policy toward the Plains Indians "genocide"? Explain.

● How might political corruption and confusion in the East, especially in Washington, affect government policies in the territories of the Great Plains and the Southwest?

Other Ethnic Minority Groups

The 1870's was a period when a number of ethnic minorities suffered. The turbulent expansion of the nation encouraged exploitation of or indifference toward poorer and ethnically differing groups. The black in the South was abandoned when Reconstruction ended. He was the victim of exploitation and oppression. The Indian was killed or herded into reservations. Another group that suffered was the Mexican American. In the areas

Chinese immigrant labor helped to build our railroads in the mid-nineteenth century

U.S. Population, 1850-80

Year	Population	Percentage increase over preceding decade
1850	23 million	35.9
1860	31 ½ million	35.6
1870	38 ½ million	22.6
1880	50 million	30.1

annexed as a result of the Treaty of Guadalupe Hidalgo (1848), many thousands of former Mexican citizens were now living on American soil. Most of them spoke little or no English. English-speaking settlers, with English-speaking governments, moved in. New governmental institutions, new laws, new courts appeared. Despite the terms of the treaty that ended the Mexican War, many Mexican American families lost their lands and rights.

Meanwhile, large numbers of Chinese laborers immigrated to the Far West to work on railroad construction. Some 160,000 Chinese were brought in by railroad builders. However, racial hostility on the part of white Americans made their lives difficult. Riots and agitation led to the passage of the Chinese Exclusion Act in 1882.

★ Find out about the anti-Chinese riots in San Francisco, 1877.

Prejudice against other immigrant groups flourished in the East and parts of the Midwest. However, the worst phase was over for the Irish, Swedish, and German immigrants.

New ethnic and economic problems were just beginning to emerge, however. In 1865 the custom of importing *contract labor* to work in the new factories was introduced. An American employer would agree to pay the transatlantic fare for any European worker who contracted to repay the fare by working up to 12 months. Many more immigrants from Europe paid their own way. These immigrants provided a supply of cheap labor that assisted industrial development, but they were bitterly resented by native American workers.

Thus began a new vast wave of immigration. This wave, called the *new immigration*, began soon after 1880. Most of these immigrants came from eastern and southern Europe. The new immigration brought major challenges of adjustment and assimilation for the generation of 1880–1910.

● How would you explain the prejudice against, and the unfair treatment of, Mexican Americans and Chinese Americans? What is ethnic prejudice? What is racial prejudice?

● Certain groups of immigrants were usually *assimilated* in the course of two or three generations. Other groups, and many indigenous Americans, seemed incapable of being assimilated. Which ethnic groups would you classify as *assimilable* and which as relatively hard to assimilate? What factors affect your classification? Is assimilation necessarily good? What alternative social processes or policies are possible?

The Beginning of a New Era

When a society undergoes many rapid changes, troubles cannot be avoided. It is therefore easy, as we look back at the 1870's, to see a great many problems in the United States. The problems would not have been present — or obvious — but for the explosive progress that Americans were making.

Just as England led the world a hundred years earlier in the First Industrial Revolution, so the United States led the Second Industrial Revolution. Just as England discovered many social, political, and economic problems in the process of industrialization, so the United States discovered problems as the Second Industrial Revolution gathered speed. In America, moreover, the problems were made more complicated by westward expansion, by massive immigration and ethnic pluralism, and by the aftermath of a terrible civil war.

● Look at the chart on page C-181. By what proportion did population increase during these three decades? What socio-economic phenomena would you expect as a result?

● Look at the list on page C-182. Was the GNP increasing as fast as or faster than population?

● In view of the facts and statistics in the charts and lists on pages C-183–C-184, what changes in the ways of life of the American people probably occurred between 1850 and 1880? Did the population become more mobile? Do you think homes were lighted better and more cheaply at the end of the period?

Some Examples of Increased Production in the United States

1. In 1840, the United States was dependent on imports for basic manufactured goods. By 1870, manufacturing had appeared in almost every industry. By 1880, the United States manufactured more goods than any other country in the world.

2. Between 1845 and 1880, United States copper output rose from 100 tons a year to 27,000 tons.

3. Between 1859 (the first oil well) and 1870, United States petroleum output rose from 2,000 barrels a year to 5.3 million barrels.

4. By 1850 mass production and interchangeable parts were so common in the United States that they were called the "American System" in the rest of the world.

5. From 1839 to 1879 the GNP of the United States grew at 4.3 per cent each year.

Miles of Railroad in America, 1850-70

1850	9,021 miles
1860	30,626 miles
1870	52,922 miles
1880	93,262 miles

How fast did news spread in 1850 and in the 1870's? What proportion of people lived in sizable towns or cities in 1850 and in 1880?

● Look at the chart on page C-187, and compare the list of examples of increased production. What do these suggest about the availability of basic and newly invented consumer goods during the period? What do they suggest about the growth of the economy? About opportunities for work or investment?

The changes in the way people lived became much more obvious after 1880. The period 1850–80 was in some ways an "interruption" in American history. People were occupied by major political problems: fighting a war, reconstructing the South, and opening up the Great Plains. Reform movements of the early Democratic period slowed down or were sidetracked.

The women's rights movement went on quietly after 1850. Before that year, six states had abolished the English common law rule that married women could not hold property apart from their husbands. Between 1860 and 1880 a number of women's colleges were added to Oberlin and Mount Holyoke. Vassar, Wellesley, Smith, Radcliffe, and Bryn Mawr were opened. Many state universities and most high schools became coeducational. Clara Barton during the war took the lead in organizing nursing services for the Union wounded and sick. She later established the American Red Cross. Susan B. Anthony and Elizabeth Cady Stanton were leaders in the movements for women's rights, and also in the temperance movement and the agitation for votes for blacks (women as well as men). The author Louisa May Alcott served as a nurse during the war, edited a children's magazine, and published her famous book, *Little Women*, in 1868–69.

There was much work still to be done in the field of social reform. The black in the North, as well as in the South, suffered from racial prejudice. Little was achieved during these years, apart from the right to public education. Public schools in most states, however, were racially segregated. Massachusetts abolished legal segregation in 1855, but other Northern states were slow to follow this example. New York City schools were legally segregated until 1900. Still, the right to education for all children was accepted in all states, and public high schools as well as elementary schools were set up in most communities.

Communication in America, 1847-66

1847	Electric telegraph linked New York and other cities of the Northeast, and Chicago and Detroit
1861	Electric telegraph from east to west coast
1866	First transatlantic cable

Growth of Cities, 1850-80*

Urban	1850		1880	
	No. of cities or towns	Actual population	No. of cities or towns	Actual population
Total urban		3,543,716		14,129,735
Cities over 1 million	—	—	1	1,206,299
500,000-1 million	1	515,547	3	1,917,018
250,000-500,000	—	—	4	1,300,809
100,000-250,000	5	659,121	12	1,786,783
50,000-100,000	4	284,355	15	947,918
25,000- 50,000	16	611,328	42	1,446,366
10,000- 25,000	36	560,783	146	2,189,447
5,000- 10,000	85	596,086	249	1,717,146
2,500- 5,000	89	316,496	467	1,617,949
Rural				
Total Rural	—	19,648,160	—	36,026,048

*Source: U.S. Bureau of the Census, *Historical Statistics of the United States, Colonial Times to 1957,* Washington, D.C., 1960, p. 14.

The movement toward labor unions was probably set back by the war. The waves of the new immigration may also have slowed the growth of unions. Yet the depression of the 1870's saw much labor violence. The real beginnings of labor unions came in the 1880's. Even then, the prevailing power in the economy of the United States remained for decades with "big business" — the bankers and the corporations that controlled steel, oil, railroads, and many other fields of production and distribution.

Most social and economic developments of the Second Industrial Revolution were still confused and chaotic in the 1870's. The generation of 1880–1910 inherited plenty of challenges from their fathers and mothers who had lived through the decade of crises, the war, Reconstruction and the turmoil of the 1870's.

Contradictions Inside the New Age

The 1870's marked the dawn of a

new age in history. Faint hints of that dawn had appeared with the scientific and industrial revolutions in Europe, but the unity of *applied science* and *industrial techniques* occurred in the United States in the 1870's and succeeding decades. In those amazing years, a new way of life and a new society came into being. Security and luxury, labor-saving devices that gave leisure, new forms of communication, and transportation and mass communication began to become available to millions and millions of persons. Goods and services hitherto available only to the wealthy (or to nobody at all) began to be at the disposal of people of ordinary means.

The products of the new industry were not, however, widely distributed at first. The period of economic expansion was also a period of hardship and poverty for many people. Ethnic and racial minorities often found life harder than ever, as wealth and comfort increased. Workers in factories and workshops did not receive a fair share of the profits on their work. Hours of work were long. Wages were low. In many states women and children drudged in factories. Unemployment was always a threat. Housing conditions were often miserable and unhealthy. Many movements of protest in the latter part of the nineteenth century prove how much discontent accompanied the Second Industrial Revolution.

● The age that dawned in the 1870's has been called by many names: the *Age of Enterprise*, the *Age of Exploitation*, the *Age of the Robber Barons*, the *Age of the Captains of Industry*, the *Gilded Age*, the *Age of Laissez Faire*. Which of these titles would you choose? Why?

● It has been said that the difference between the First Industrial Revolution and the Second Industrial Revolution is this: the First Industrial Revolution brought cheap and abundant production of goods that people had been using for centuries; the Second Industrial Revolution brought new, unprecedented goods into production and made people want them. Do you agree? Give examples of the two types of goods.

● We are still living in an age of industrial revolution. What are some problems or challenges it brought that are still unsolved or unsettled?

★ What is the connection between the Second Industrial Revolution and the *revolution of rising expectations* in developing countries? How did industry and science affect population trends in the world?

★ What was the Marxist analysis of capitalism? How would a Marxist criticize the "Age of Enterprise"? What predictions might he make about the future of America?

● The theory of *laissez faire* was largely accepted in the United States at this time. What is *laissez faire*? What major exception to the theory was obvious in the 1860's–70's? Does the theory account in part for the helplessness and corruption of the United States government in social and economic matters? Explain.

● Here are some remarks made by successful businessmen in the 1870's. What do they suggest about their philosophy? James J. Hill (successful railroad builder and financier):

If you want to know whether you are destined to be a success or a failure in life, you can easily find out. The test is simple and infallible. Are you able to save money? If not, drop out. You will lose.

J.P. Morgan (powerful financier):

Well, I don't know as I want a lawyer to tell me what I cannot do. I hire him to tell me how to do what I want to do.

John D. Rockefeller (multimillionaire entrepreneur, founder of Standard Oil):

The ability to deal with people is as purchasable a commodity as sugar or coffee. And I pay more for that ability than for any other under the sun.[5]

★ Who was Horatio Alger? In what ways are his writings typical of this period (c. 1870–90)? In what ways might they be misleading?

---

[5]The quotations from Hill, Morgan, and Rockefeller, are taken from Clifton Fadiman (ed.), *The American Treasury 1455–1955* (New York: Harper, 1955), pp. 701 and 183.

(Above) An angry John P. Morgan, financier

(Right) Cornelius "Commodore" Vanderbilt, railroad tycoon

Some American Inventions, 1846-80

1846	The rotary printing press
1848	First milling machine for mass production of light metal goods
1850	Singer's sewing machine
1852	First passenger elevator
1858	Shoe-sewing machine
1860	The Winchester repeating rifle
1862	The Gatling machine gun
1865-75	Web printing press
1867	First practical typewriter
1869	First suction type vacuum cleaner
	Celluloid manufactured
	Electric voting machine
1870-78	Motion pictures began
1872	Calculating machines
1874	Electric streetcar
	Barbed wire
1875	First dynamo for outdoor lighting
1876	Telephone
1878	Phonograph
1878-83	Electric lighting: incandescent lamp
1880	First roll film for cameras
	Safety razor
1877-80's	Agricultural machines: spring-tooth harrow, twine binder, gang plow, combine harvester-thresher, and others

Conclusion

The problems of 1850 must have seemed very far away and almost forgotten to someone looking back from the year 1880. Those problems, in the main, had been so definitively, and even brutally, settled that it was difficult to remember that they once looked so grave and insoluble. Slavery — sectional rivalry — fire-eating pro-slavery Southern politicians — bleeding Kansas: all these had gone with the great wind of war that had swept through the South.

With the war itself many new challenges emerged. It was a new kind of war, devastating and cruel, fought by mass armies, with rifles and heavy artillery, relying on railroads for swift transport of men and supplies. In the long run the sheer weight of the North's supremacy in resources brought the Confederacy to unconditional surrender.

Then came the problems of the peace. The assassination of Lincoln coupled with the Black Codes passed by Southern legislatures that seemed to have learned nothing from defeat led to the triumph of the Radical Republicans. From the moderation of presidential Reconstruction, the Union turned to the coercion of congressional Reconstruction. Strenuous efforts to force racial equality on the South in the end led to reaction. Northern enthusiasm died out, and harsh white supremacy was restored in the solidly Democratic South. The sufferings of black Americans had not been abolished along with slavery.

Meanwhile, in the North and West vast changes had also occurred. In politics the firm principles that had marked the Republican party evaporated. Opportunism and graft marked the presidency of Ulysses S. Grant, and compromise and inaction the presidency of Rutherford B. Hayes. In fact, the energies of the nation were turned away from politics. Technological improvement, industrial expansion, financial speculation, railroad building, settling the Great Plains, cattle driving and wheat farming, all of these things provided outlets for the ambitions and energies of the American people. The new generation coming into its own in the 1870's faced a future of unprecedented opportunity and completely new problems and challenges — a future of turbulence and power. That new generation shaped the America we live in today.

● As you review the period 1850–80, what great changes in public opinion or public attitudes do you notice? How would you explain them? Would you say they show a *dialectical* pattern — a swing from one extreme to another?

★ You may wish to study the biography of some interesting figure of the period. Here are some suggestions: John Brown, Clara Barton, Frederick Douglass, Thaddeus Stevens, Charles Sumner, Herman Melville, Elizabeth Cady Stanton, Sojourner Truth, Judah P. Benjamin, Ralph Waldo Emerson, Harriet Beecher Stowe, Samuel Langhorne Clemens (Mark Twain), Winslow Homer, Emily Dickinson, Julia Ward Howe, Fanny Fern, John Ericsson. There are many more. It was a time that allowed room for colorful individuals.

★ The success of the Union gave the United States and its institutions

U.S. History, 1850-80

1850	Clay's compromise Admission of California Death of President Taylor Millard Fillmore became president
1852	*Uncle Tom's Cabin* Election of Franklin Pierce as president
1854	Kansas-Nebraska Act Republican party founded Ostend Manifesto
1855	"Bleeding" Kansas
1856	John Brown's Pottawatomie Massacre Beating of Charles Sumner Election of James Buchanan as president
1857	*Dred Scott* decision
1858	Lincoln-Douglas Debates
1859	John Brown at Harpers Ferry
1860	Election of Abraham Lincoln as president Secession of South Carolina
1861	Secession of seven states of Lower South Confederate States of America established Morrill Tariff Act
Apr.	Attack on Fort Sumter Lincoln calls for troops States of the Upper South secede
July	1st battle of Bull Run
Feb.	Union victories in Tennessee
1862 Apr.	Battle of Shiloh: Union takes Memphis Farragut takes New Orleans Peninsula campaign in Virginia
May	Homestead Act
June-July	Seven Days' Battle: McClellan retreats
Aug.	2nd battle of Bull Run
Sept.	Antietam: Lee withdraws from Maryland
1863 Jan.	Emancipation Proclamation
May	Chancellorsville: Lee victorious
July	Fall of Vicksburg Gettysburg: Lee withdraws

	Chattanooga taken by the North
1864 May	Battle of the Wilderness
May-Sept.	Sherman's march through Georgia
June	Cold Harbor
	Petersburg
Nov.	Sherman's march to the sea
	Reelection of Lincoln
Dec.	Battle of Nashville
1865 Apr.	Lee surrenders at Appomattox
	Assassination of Lincoln
May-July	President Andrew Johnson's Reconstruction proclamations
Nov.	Black Codes in Southern states
Dec.	13th Amendment
1866	Radical Republicans organize and gain control of Congress
	14th Amendment introduced (ratified 1868)
1867-68	Reconstruction acts
	Military rule in South
	Reconstruction governments begin
	Purchase of Alaska
1868 Feb.-May	Impeachment of Johnson
	Election of Ulysses S. Grant as president
1869	Gould and Fisk's "corner in gold"
	Completion of first transcontinental railroad
1870	Ku Klux Klan
	Grant tries to annex Santo Domingo
1871	Tweed Ring scandal
	Series of Apache wars begin
1872	Credit Mobilier scandal
	Reelection of Grant despite Liberal Republican movement
1873	Financial panic
1875	Whisky Ring scandal
	2nd Sioux War (Little Bighorn, June 1876)
1876-77	Election of Rutherford B. Hayes as president after long dispute over votes
	End of Reconstruction
	Defeat of the Nez Percé
1880	Election of James A. Garfield as president

great prestige in the world. Democracy had proved capable of surviving the terrible strain of civil war. Find out how democratic reforms were introduced in Britain (1867 and 1884), France (1871–75), Spain (1869–76), Italy (1881), Switzerland (1874), Germany (1871), Japan (1889), Brazil (1881), Russia (1864, 1870). Not all of these reforms led to immediate popular representative government, but they proved that governments had to pay at least "lip service" to democracy. Democracy spread in many nations besides those mentioned in this question.

★ What had been happening in the rest of the world during this period? There were, for example, other wars and movements for national unity and independence in Germany, Italy, the Austrian Empire, and Mexico. What happened to slavery in Russia and Brazil? What war was fought in Europe in 1854–56? In 1870–71? What rebellion occurred in India in 1857? In China, 1850–64? What happened in Japan in 1854? What foreign intervention took place in Mexico and how did it end? What great canal was opened in 1869?

(Left) The last moment of Maximilian, Emperor of Mexico

Commodore Perry visited Japan, March 8, 1854

Nineteenth century reformers, authors, abolitionists, and women who fought for suffrage. (clockwise from the top) Lucretia Mott, E. Cady Stanton, Mary A. Livermore, Lydia Marie Child, Susan B. Anthony, Grace Greenwood, and in the center, Anna E. Dickinson

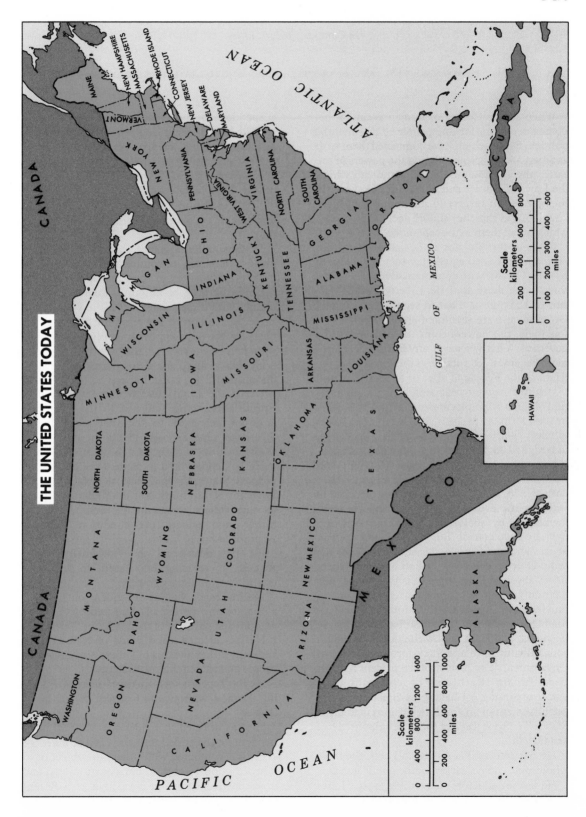

THE UNITED STATES TODAY

THE DECLARATION OF INDEPENDENCE

In Congress, July 4, 1776

THE UNANIMOUS DECLARATION OF THE THIRTEEN UNITED STATES OF AMERICA

When in the Course of human events, it becomes necessary for one people to dissolve the political bands which have connected them with another, and to assume among the powers of the earth, the separate and equal station to which the Laws of Nature and of Nature's God entitle them, a decent respect to the opinions of mankind requires that they should declare the causes which impel them to the separation.

We hold these truths to be self-evident, that all men are created equal, that they are endowed by their Creator with certain unalienable Rights, that among these are Life, Liberty and the pursuit of Happiness. That to secure these rights, Governments are instituted among Men, deriving their just powers from the consent of the governed; That whenever any Form of Government becomes destructive of these ends it is the Right of the People to alter or to abolish it, and to institute new Government, laying its foundation on such principles and organizing its powers in such form, as to them shall seem most likely to effect their Safety and Happiness. Prudence, indeed, will dictate that Governments long established should not be changed for light and transient causes; and accordingly all experience hath shown, that mankind are more disposed to suffer, while evils are sufferable, than to right themselves by abolishing the forms to which they are accustomed. But when a long train of abuses and usurpations, pursuing invariably the same Objects evinces a design to reduce them under absolute Despotism, it is their right, it is their duty, to throw off such Government, and to provide new Guards for their future security. — Such has been the patient sufferance of these Colonies; and such is now the necessity which constrains them to alter their former Systems of Government. The history of the present King of Great Britain is a history of repeated injuries and usurpations, all having in direct object the establishment of an absolute Tyranny over these States. To prove this, let Facts be submitted to a candid world.

He has refused his Assent to Laws, the most wholesome and necessary for the public good.

He has forbidden his Governors to pass Laws of immediate and pressing importance, unless suspended in their operation till his Assent should be obtained; and when so suspended, he has utterly neglected to attend to them.

He has refused to pass other Laws for the accommodation of large districts of people, unless those people would relinquish the right of Representation in the Legislature, a right inestimable to them and formidable to tyrants only.

He has called together legislative bodies at places unusual, uncomfortable, and distant from the depository of their public records, for the sole purpose of fatiguing them into compliance with his measures.

He has dissolved Representative Houses repeatedly, for opposing with manly firmness his invasions on the rights of the people.

He has refused for a long time, after such dissolutions, to cause others to be elected; whereby the Legislative powers, incapable of Annihilation, have returned to the People at large for their exercise; the State remaining in the mean time exposed to all the dangers of invasions from without, and convulsions within.

He has endeavored to prevent the population of these States; for that purpose obstructing the Laws for Naturalization of Foreigners; refusing to pass others to encourage their migration hither, and raising the conditions of new Appropriations of Lands.

He has obstructed the Administration of Justice, by refusing his Assent to Laws for establishing Judiciary powers.

He has made Judges dependent on his Will alone for the tenure of their offices, and the amount and payment of their salaries.

He has erected a multitude of New Offices, and sent hither swarms of Officers to harass our people and eat out their substance.

He has kept among us in times of peace, Standing Armies, without the Consent of our legislatures.

He has affected to render the Military independent of, and superior to, the Civil power.

He has combined with others to subject us to a jurisdiction foreign to our constitutions, and unacknowledged by our laws; giving his Assent to their Acts of pretended Legislation:

For quartering large bodies of armed troops among us;

For protecting them, by a mock Trial, from punishment for any Murders which they should commit on the Inhabitants of these States;

For cutting off our Trade with all parts of the world;

For imposing Taxes on us without our Consent;

For depriving us, in many cases, of the benefits of Trial by Jury;

For transporting us beyond Seas, to be tried for pretended offenses;

For abolishing the free System of English Laws in a neighboring Province, establishing therein an Arbitrary government, and enlarging its Boundaries, so as to render it at once an example and fit instrument for introducing the same absolute rule into these Colonies;

For taking away our Charters, abolishing our most valuable Laws, and altering, fundamentally, the Forms of our Governments;

For suspending our own Legislatures, and declaring themselves invested with Power to legislate for us in all cases whatsoever.

He has abdicated Government here, by declaring us out of his Protection, and waging War against us.

He has plundered our seas, ravaged our Coasts, burned our towns, and destroyed the lives of our people.

He is at this time transporting large Armies of foreign Mercenaries to complete the works of death, desolation and tyranny, already begun with circumstances of Cruelty and perfidy scarcely paralleled in the most barbarous ages, and totally unworthy the Head of a civilized nation.

He has constrained our fellow Citizens taken Captive on the high Seas to bear Arms against their Country, to become the executioners of their friends and Brethren, or to fall themselves by their Hands.

He has excited domestic insurrections amongst us, and has endeavored to bring on the inhabitants of our frontiers the merciless Indian Savages whose known rule of warfare is an undistinguished destruction of all ages, sexes, and conditions.

In every stage of these Oppressions We have Petitioned for Redress in the most humble terms. Our repeated Petitions have been answered only by repeated injury. A Prince whose character is thus marked by every act which may define a Tyrant, is unfit to be the ruler of a free people.

Nor have We been wanting in attentions to our British brethren. We have warned them from time to time of attempts by their legislature to extend an unwarrantable jurisdiction over us. We have reminded them of the circumstances of our emigration and settlement here. We have appealed to their native justice and magnanimity, and we have conjured them by the ties of our common kindred to disavow these usurpations, which, would inevitably interrupt our connections and correspondence. They too have been deaf to the voice of justice and of consanguinity. We must, therefore, acquiesce in the necessity, which denounces our Separation, and hold them, as we hold the rest of mankind, Enemies in War, in Peace Friends. —

We, therefore, the Representatives of the United States of America, in General Congress, Assembled, appealing to the Supreme Judge of the world for the rectitude of our intentions, do, in the Name, and by the Authority of the good People of these Colonies, solemnly publish and declare, That these United Colonies are, and of right ought to be Free and Independent States; that they are Absolved from all Allegiance to the British Crown, and that all political connection between them and the State of Great Britain, is and ought to be totally dissolved, and that as Free and Independent States, they have full Power to levy War, conclude Peace, contract Alliances, establish Commerce, and to do all other Acts and Things which Independent States may of right do. And for the support of this Declaration, with a firm reliance on the protection of Divine Providence, we mutually pledge to each other our Lives, our Fortunes and our sacred Honor.

JOHN HANCOCK

other signers

PRESIDENTS AND VICE-PRESIDENTS
OF THE UNITED STATES OF AMERICA

No.	President		State	Years in Office	Party	Vice-President
1	George Washington	(1732-1799)	Va.	1789-1797		John Adams
2	John Adams	(1735-1826)	Mass.	1797-1801	Federalist	Thomas Jefferson
3	Thomas Jefferson	(1743-1826)	Va.	1801-1809	Democratic-Republican	Aaron Burr George Clinton
4	James Madison	(1751-1836)	Va.	1809-1817	Dem.-Rep.	George Clinton Elbridge Gerry
5	James Monroe	(1758-1831)	Va.	1817-1825	Dem.-Rep.	Daniel D. Tompkins
6	John Quincy Adams	(1767-1848)	Mass.	1825-1829	Dem.-Rep.	John C. Calhoun
7	Andrew Jackson	(1767-1845)	Tenn.	1829-1837	Democratic	John C. Calhoun Martin Van Buren
8	Martin Van Buren	(1782-1862)	N.Y.	1837-1841	Democratic	Richard M. Johnson
9	William H. Harrison	(1773-1841)	Ohio	1841	Whig	John Tyler
10	John Tyler	(1790-1862)	Va.	1841-1845	Whig	
11	James K. Polk	(1795-1849)	Tenn.	1845-1849	Democratic	George M. Dallas
12	Zachary Taylor	(1784-1850)	La.	1849-1850	Whig	Millard Fillmore
13	Millard Fillmore	(1800-1874)	N.Y.	1850-1853	Whig	
14	Franklin Pierce	(1804-1869)	N.H.	1853-1857	Democratic	William R. King
15	James Buchanan	(1791-1868)	Pa.	1857-1861	Democratic	John C. Breckinridge
16	Abraham Lincoln	(1809-1865)	Ill.	1861-1865	Republican	Hannibal Hamlin Andrew Johnson
17	Andrew Johnson	(1808-1875)	Tenn.	1865-1869	Republican	
18	Ulysses S. Grant	(1822-1885)	Ill.	1869-1877	Republican	Schuyler Colfax Henry Wilson
19	Rutherford B. Hayes	(1822-1893)	Ohio	1877-1881	Republican	William A. Wheeler
20	James A. Garfield	(1831-1881)	Ohio	1881	Republican	Chester A. Arthur
21	Chester A. Arthur	(1830-1886)	N.Y.	1881-1885	Republican	
22	Grover Cleveland	(1837-1908)	N.Y.	1885-1889	Democratic	Thomas A. Hendricks
23	Benjamin Harrison	(1833-1901)	Ind.	1889-1893	Republican	Levi P. Morton
24	Grover Cleveland	(1837-1908)	N.Y.	1893-1897	Democratic	Adlai E. Stevenson
25	William McKinley	(1843-1901)	Ohio	1897-1901	Republican	Garret A. Hobart Theodore Roosevelt
26	Theodore Roosevelt	(1858-1919)	N.Y.	1901-1909	Republican	Charles W. Fairbanks
27	William H. Taft	(1857-1930)	Ohio	1909-1913	Republican	James S. Sherman
28	Woodrow Wilson	(1856-1924)	N.J.	1913-1921	Democratic	Thomas R. Marshall
29	Warren G. Harding	(1865-1923)	Ohio	1921-1923	Republican	Calvin Coolidge
30	Calvin Coolidge	(1872-1933)	Mass.	1923-1929	Republican	Charles G. Dawes
31	Herbert Hoover	(1874-1964)	Calif.	1929-1933	Republican	Charles Curtis
32	Franklin D. Roosevelt	(1882-1945)	N.Y.	1933-1945	Democratic	John N. Garner Henry A. Wallace Harry S Truman
33	Harry S. Truman	(1884-1972)	Mo.	1945-1953	Democratic	Alben W. Barkley
34	Dwight D. Eisenhower	(1890-1969)	N.Y.	1953-1961	Republican	Richard M. Nixon
35	John F. Kennedy	(1917-1963)	Mass.	1961-1963	Democratic	Lyndon B. Johnson
36	Lyndon B. Johnson	(1908-1973)	Texas	1963-1969	Democratic	Hubert H. Humphrey
37	Richard M. Nixon	(1913-)	Calif.	1969-1974	Republican	Spiro T. Agnew Gerald R. Ford
38	Gerald R. Ford	(1913-)	Mich.	1974-	Republican	Nelson A. Rockefeller